THEY
CALL ME
A HERO

THEY CALL ME A HERO

A MEMOIR OF MY YOUTH

DANIEL HERNANDEZ
with SUSAN GOLDMAN RUBIN

FOREWORD BY
DEBBIE WASSERMAN SCHULTZ, MEMBER OF CONGRESS

SIMON & SCHUSTER BFYR

NEW YORK LONDON TORONTO SYDNEY NEW DELHI

SIMON & SCHUSTER BFYR

An imprint of Simon & Schuster Children's Publishing Division

1230 Avenue of the Americas, New York, New York 10020

This work is a memoir. It reflects the author's present recollections of his experiences over a period of years.

SIMON & SCHUSTER BFYR is a trademark of Simon & Schuster, Inc.

For information about special discounts for bulk purchases, please contact Simon & Schuster Special Sales at 1-866-506-1949 or business@simonandschuster.com.

The Simon & Schuster Speakers Bureau can bring authors to your live event. For more information or to book an event, contact the Simon & Schuster Speakers Bureau at 1-866-248-3049 or visit our website at www.simonspeakers.com.

Book design by Chloë Foglia

The text for this book is set in Granjon.

Manufactured in the United States of America

10 9 8 7 6 5 4 3 2 1

Library of Congress Cataloging-in-Publication Data

Hernandez, Daniel, 1990–

They call me a hero : a memoir of my youth / Daniel Hernandez and Susan Goldman Rubin. — 1st ed.

p. cm.

ISBN 978-1-4424-6228-1 (hardcover) — ISBN 978-1-4424-6238-0 (ebook)

1. Hernandez, Daniel, 1990—Juvenile literature. 2. Giffords, Gabrielle D. (Gabrielle Dee), 1970—Friends and associates—Juvenile literature. 3. Interns—United States—Biography—Juvenile literature. 4. Giffords, Gabrielle D. (Gabrielle Dee), 1970—Assassination attempt, 2011—Juvenile literature. 5. Heroes—Arizona—Tucson—Biography—Juvenile literature. 6. Courage—Arizona—Tucson—History—21st century—Juvenile literature. 7. Tucson (Ariz.)—History—21st century—Juvenile literature. 8. Tucson (Ariz.)—Officials and employees—Biography—Juvenile literature. 9. Sexual minorities—Civil rights—Arizona—Tucson—Juvenile literature. I. Rubin, Susan Goldman. II. Title.

E901.1.H46A3 2013

979.1'054092—dc23

[B]

2012019829

FIRST EDITION

To the victims of January 8, 2011, in memory of Christina-Taylor Green, Dorothy Morris, John Roll, Phyllis Schneck, Dorwan Stoddard, and Gabriel Zimmerman, and in memory of Daniel's dear uncles Art Hernandez and Marcos Quiñones

—D. H. and S. G. R.

CONTENTS

Foreword

BY DEBBIE WASSERMAN SCHULTZ, MEMBER OF CONGRESS

A LOT CAN BE AND HAS BEEN SAID ABOUT AMERICAN DEMOCRACY. For more than two centuries it has been rightly held up as a model for new democracies and aspiring peoples across the globe who yearn to experience what it is to be free.

We are taught in school that American democracy is about principles: one person, one vote; equal protection under the law; life, liberty, and the pursuit of happiness. But while the selection of our leaders through a nonviolent expression of the people is a fundamental aspect of our democratic system, it is only the end result of a long process that speaks even more profoundly of the participatory character of our democracy. Ask any president, senator, representative, city councilperson, or school board member how they got to where they are today, and they'll tell you that they wouldn't have achieved their goals without the volunteer help of everyday Americans. Every name you see on the ballot, every candidate at a debate, or any politician you see on TV owes their success in no small part to the passion and dedication of everyday, ordinary Americans.

Each year hundreds of thousands of Americans volunteer for a political campaign, or a political organization, or a ballot initiative. Whether they gather petitions to get a candidate or a cause on the ballot, answer phones in an office, walk door-to-door to promote their candidate, register voters, or work as a nonpartisan poll worker, these volunteers and their countless hours of unpaid work are the backbone of America's democracy.

Some volunteer because they believe in a person; others volunteer because they believe in their party. Some because they see parallels in a candidate's platform with a personal cause or that of a loved one; and some just believe it is their civic duty. Regardless of the motivation, one thing is clear: American democracy would not function properly without them.

Daniel Hernandez, a veteran volunteer of both Hillary Clinton's presidential campaign and Congresswoman Gabby Giffords's 2008 reelection campaign, had signed up in 2011 to once again volunteer for Congresswoman Giffords, this time as an intern in her Tucson, Arizona, congressional office. America got to know Daniel Hernandez as the young intern who rushed to Gabby's side immediately following her being shot that horrible morning. I am eternally grateful for Daniel and everyone who played a role in saving the life of my friend that day, but that is not why I write this foreword.

Much has been written about how Gabby was shot while doing exactly what our Founding Fathers envisioned for a participatory democracy, a forum through which everyday Americans could talk, face-to-face, with their local member of Congress. But gaining less attention was the work of the others who were there that morning, the people without whom Gabby would never have been elected to Congress, nor be able to perform the job of Congressperson. They are the staffers, one of whom lost his life and others of whom were injured—both physically and mentally—and Daniel Hernandez, who was less than one week into his unpaid internship in Gabby's congressional office. These public servants were simply doing their jobs that Saturday morning, helping Tucsonans meet with their congressperson. Just as Daniel's story neither begins nor ends at the shooting in Tucson, neither does the importance of using his story to better understand America.

Anyone who meets Daniel is struck by three things: his confidence, his calmness, and his determination. Yet for too many Americans even today, Daniel, as an openly gay, Hispanic young man, should never have been there that Saturday morning. For them, Daniel's sexual orientation and ethnicity disqualify him—they represent something wrong with society, an America that is forgetting its roots. And that is why Daniel's story—the complete story—is worthy of reflection.

America, the great melting pot, the standard by which all

other democracies are judged, was originally colonized by white men who believed that only white, land-owning men should have the right to vote. Over the centuries, and not without struggle and intense internal debate, America has evolved, and I believe now more fully embraces the spirit of inclusive participatory democracy than could have been imagined at the birth of our nation. Yet change is difficult and, for some, harder to accept than for others.

On Saturday, January 8, 2011, Daniel Hernandez was doing what hundreds of thousands of Americans do every year: He was volunteering for a person that he believed in. But then he did something that we all wonder whether we'd instinctively have the courage to do ourselves: He heard gunshots and ran toward them, to help those in need. His actions that day helped to save my friend's life and they helped every American see the sharp contrast between the evil displayed by a deranged shooter and the selflessness of individuals who rushed in to help those in need.

Daniel's story exemplifies the point that American exceptionalism is rooted in individual freedom and liberty, a notion that welcomes everyone from all paths of life into the American experience. Simply put: excluding Daniel that fateful Saturday wouldn't have hurt him nearly as much as it would have hurt America.

I hope that you enjoy getting to know Daniel as much as I have.

Representative Debbie Wasserman Schultz, Daniel, and
Daniel's mother in Washington, DC, February 2011

PART ONE

~ THE SHOOTING ~

Chapter One
Saturday Morning

"Gun!" someone said, and it clicked: I remembered some of the things that had happened over the past several months. There had been a campaign event where an angry constituent had brought a gun but had dropped it. And the door of Gabby Giffords's congressional office in Tucson had been shot at last March, after the vote on health care. Gabe Zimmerman, Gabby's aide, had come up to me that morning and said, "If you see anything suspicious, let me know."

So I heard shots, and the first thing I thought of was Gabby—making sure she was okay. I was about thirty to forty feet away from the congresswoman. I heard the shots and ran toward the sound.

I don't consider myself a hero. I did what I thought anyone should have done. Heroes are people who spend a lifetime committed to helping others. I was just a twenty-year-old intern who happened to be in the right place at the right time.

That Saturday, January 8, 2011, started like an ordinary day. I got dressed in business casual clothes: shirt, argyle sweater, khakis—what I wear to the office. Gabe Zimmerman had organized a Congress on Your Corner event at a shopping center just north of Tucson. Representative Giffords liked to meet her constituents in person and talk to them about what was on their minds, and discuss what was happening in Congress that they were concerned about. Weeks before, I had applied for an internship at her office, and they had accepted me halfway through the interview. I was supposed to start on January 12, when school was scheduled to begin. I'm a student at the University of Arizona and major in political science. But the office was short-staffed, and I'd volunteered to start early.

I had known Gabby for years. I'd worked on her campaigns since I'd met her in June 2008. She's the kindest, warmest individual you will ever meet. "I don't do handshakes, honey," she always says. "I do hugs."

Gabe had asked me to be at the Safeway market at the corner of Ina and Oracle by nine a.m. to help with the setup. By mistake I went to the wrong Safeway and didn't get to the right one till nine thirty. Everyone else on staff was already there, and they were almost done with setting up folding tables and a few chairs in front of the store. I put a sandwich board outside the market near the entrance that advertised the event. Then I helped Gabe hang a banner from poles that read, GABRIELLE GIFFORDS, UNITED STATES CONGRESS, and the Arizona flag and the American flag. I made sure we had pens that were actually working so people could sign in.

Ever thoughtful Gabe was the consummate social worker. He was beloved by all who knew him for his kind heart and the good head on his shoulders. He was what we called the Constituent Whisperer, because he had the uncanny ability to take even the angriest constituent and calm them down.

It was cold that morning but clear. Pam Simon, the community outreach coordinator, went into the market for coffee. Before she went she asked Gabe if he'd like anything. But Gabe said no and instead made sure to ask her if she had asked me if I wanted anything. I thought it was so incredibly sweet of Gabe to ask Pam on my behalf. Sometimes interns are forgotten in situations like this.

When constituents started arriving, they had to go through me. I was standing with my clipboard to register them at the back wall of the market close to the adjoining Walgreens drugstore. That's where they had to get in line. Gabby was about forty feet away near the entrance to the Safeway market. As people lined up waiting to speak to her, they wrote down their names, addresses, and phone numbers. We were keeping track of how many folks stopped by and how many lived in the district. I talked to everyone.

A girl named Christina-Taylor Green was there with her neighbor Suzi Hileman. Suzi signed in, and I made sure that Christina-Taylor got to sign in too, because she was so young and so excited to be meeting a congresswoman. I asked Christina-Taylor how old she was, and she told me she was nine. And I asked her what school she went to, and she said Mesa Verde Elementary. We talked briefly about her being on the student council. Then she said she wanted to ask Gabby a question, but she didn't want to ask something stupid and needed help. We had information on the table that had been issued, in the form of press releases, on the accomplishments of the congresswoman. Even though it was way over Christina-Taylor's head, I gave her copies of three different press releases.

Then I went to the back of the line to continue registering people.

Gabe had set up stanchions, the metal poles with polyester bands that are used at banks to help customers form lines. He liked to have them at events so that we had a clearly defined entry and a clearly defined exit. There were chairs against the brick wall where those at the very front could sit before speaking to the congresswoman.

At 9:55 Gabby pulled up in her car. At ten o'clock she greeted everyone and said, "Thank you for being with us on a chilly Saturday morning." She wore a bright red jacket. Gabe stood nearby in case a constituent were to ask for help from the office. Ron Barber, Gabby's dedicated district director, stood at her side as well, listening and watching proudly as his boss carefully and adeptly talked with constituents. Jim and Doris Tucker were at the head of the line, but the first person who actually spoke to her was Judge John Roll. He had stopped by to say hello. Then she talked to the Tuckers and Dorwan and Mavy Stoddard.

Meanwhile, at the back of the line, I checked in Bill Badger, a retired army colonel. Although he was a Republican and Gabby was a Democrat, he admired her and knew she would answer his questions.

I had just checked in Bill Badger when I heard what I thought was gunfire. It was 10:10 a.m. For about half a second I thought, *Oh, maybe it's fireworks*. Then I heard someone say, "Gun!"

Chapter Two
Stop the Bleeding

There was blood everywhere. Bodies on the ground. Screams. As I rushed toward the sidewalk in front of the market, I passed the gunman. I saw him shooting with a pistol. He was running away through the entry line we had set up outside, and I was running through the exit. The whole time he was continuing to fire into the line of people who were there to see Congresswoman Giffords. He was indiscriminately shooting.

I'm big, but I didn't think of tackling him. In that split second I figured it was more useful to go to the front, where people had been injured, than to try to stop him. I didn't know how many weapons he had, and I didn't know how many rounds he had left in his magazine. It was probably not the best idea to run toward the gunshots, but people needed help. I had limited medical training in high school and knew that people could bleed out in seconds from gunshot wounds. When I went to the front, it wasn't just to find Gabby; it was to find out who was injured. I knew that Gabe and other staffers were in the vicinity too.

I checked for pulses in the two victims closest to me. First the neck, then the wrist. Gabe Zimmerman was dead. Ron Barber was on the ground bleeding. He was still conscious, and he was in shock and in a lot of pain. Ron had been shot in the leg and the face. But even at this moment he was asking me to move on and check others who needed more help. "Make sure you stay with Gabby," he said. "Make sure you go help Gabby."

I moved from person to person checking pulses. The first rule in a trauma situation is you do what you can and move on. Ron was in serious condition but not as serious as the congresswoman, who had been shot in the head and was still alert and conscious.

I saw Gabby. At first it looked as though she might be in a defensive position. I had hoped that she had been uninjured, but as I got closer, I saw that she had fallen and was lying on the sidewalk bleeding from a head wound. I quickly started looking around her body to see if there were any other visible injuries. Seeing none, I applied pressure to the entry wound on her forehead with my bare hand.

I pulled Gabby into my lap and helped her sit upright so that she wouldn't choke on her own blood. She was still alert and she was still conscious. That was a good sign. Her eyes were closed and she couldn't talk, but she was moving her right hand and using that to respond. I wanted to make sure she knew what was going on around her. I let her know she had been shot in the head and that the authorities had been alerted. My main priority was to keep her engaged, keep her calm. I kept asking her questions like, "If you understand that the ambulance is coming, squeeze my hand." And she squeezed my hand. I said, "We're going to take you to the hospital; everything's going to be okay."

While there was a lot of blood, it didn't look like she had an arterial bleed. If she'd been bleeding from an artery, she could have lost a lot of blood in a very short amount of time. Her gunshot wound was through her brain. Not too much blood is lost in that kind of injury. I had learned this in high school when I'd trained to be a nursing assistant and phlebotomist. Although the subject of trauma injuries hadn't been covered in my studies, I had had conversations about this topic with different doctors and people who worked in health care. I had asked questions about anything I thought was interesting.

So now I felt confident that I was doing the right thing for Gabby. After I had been with her for a minute or so, a couple who had been shopping in the market dashed out to help. He was a doctor and his wife was a nurse. They came over to me and checked really quickly to see what I was doing. Dr. Bowman told me to continue applying pressure to Gabby's wound. "Don't let her move around," he said. "Keep doing what you're doing."

The shooter had tried to reload, but a woman named Patricia Maisch had grabbed the clip. Roger Salzgeber, who'd been standing eight feet away from Gabby, and Bill Badger had wrestled the gunman to the ground and now held him there. I couldn't see the gunman from where I was, but the shooting had obviously stopped. It lasted only nineteen seconds, I learned later.

Pam Simon was dead. Someone looked her over and said, "She's a goner."

Sirens wailed. Minutes later police and paramedics arrived. The police secured the crime scene with yellow tape before they let the paramedics assist the victims. The police had to make sure there were no other assailants.

Gabby kept trying to move around. When the paramedics were finally allowed to come over to us, they asked me where Gabby had been shot and if there were any other injuries. There was one obvious gunshot wound to the head, but there wasn't any other injury that we knew of. First they had to immobilize her neck. So while she was still in my lap, they put a neck brace on her. They wrapped an Israeli bandage, which was used to stop the bleeding, around her forehead. She still kept moving, so they asked me to hold the gauze in place until they could get more. Then they got a stretcher and put her on it. The paramedics wanted to wait for a helicopter. "What's the ETA [estimated time of arrival]?" I asked. They said about twenty minutes. "We've got to get her out of here in the first ambulance," I yelled at them. "She's still alert and responding to commands." Everyone was in shock. There was so much confusion that it helped that I yelled. No one was giving clear instructions. So the paramedics listened when I said, This is what we're doing. I told them to take her to the hospital right away. I held her hand as they hurried her to the ambulance. "I'm going with her," I said to the paramedics.

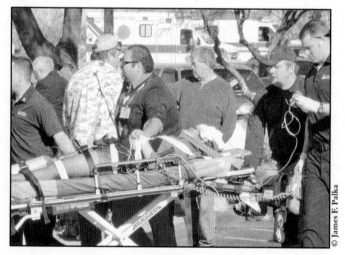

After the shooting, Daniel and the paramedics
take Gabby, on stretcher, to the ambulance.

They told me they could take only family, but I pushed my way into the ambulance. Sirens screamed as we sped along.

Gabby was in a lot of pain. They were trying to get an IV

started, but they couldn't find a vein. They poked her repeatedly. She kept writhing around. I think having me there to calm her down helped the paramedics focus on their work. I was trying to figure out what I could do at that point. I told her we were going to try to get ahold of her husband, Captain Mark Kelly, and her parents, Gloria and Spencer Giffords. But I didn't have Mark's number or her family's number. I had a new cell phone, and I hadn't had a chance to put in numbers for people I would have normally called who were involved with the Democratic Party and knew Mark and Gabby.

The only one I could think of was Steve Farley. Steve is the state representative from District 28, Tucson, and I had worked as his campaign manager. I had become friends with Steve and his wife, Kelly, and his daughters, Amelia and GiGi. And he and Gabby were friends. So I called him before I called my parents, and told him what had happened. In the background I could hear Kelly and the girls laughing and saying hello; they were on their way to Kartchner Caverns State Park. I immediately told Steve, "Steve, shut up, stop talking. Gabby's been shot. I'm in an ambulance with her. I need you to call Gloria and her husband. We are headed to UMC. HURRY." I assumed we were going to the University Medical Center because it's the only trauma center in the city of Tucson, and, in fact, all of southern Arizona.

Then I called my parents to let them know I hadn't been injured, but I didn't tell them anything besides that. I knew that they would be frightened, but I also knew that time was limited and it was more important for me to talk with Gabby to try to keep her calm on the way to the hospital. Keeping my parents and sisters informed was secondary to my job of tending to Gabby.

When we reached University Medical Center, the ambulance doors opened. The medical staff rushed Gabby into the hospital and told me to stand there and stay still. Sheriff's deputies said, "Someone will be with you shortly." They said I wasn't allowed to talk to anyone or use my cell phone or interact with anybody until the sheriff's deputies questioned me.

People had started to gather to see what was happening. Media trucks began to arrive.

My clothes were covered in blood.

CHAPTER THREE
CRIME SCENE EVIDENCE

I STOOD IN THE AMBULANCE BAY OF THE HOSPITAL, WAITING. Deputies put me in an isolation area so I could be questioned by detectives. As someone walked by, I overheard her saying that Gabby had passed away. I sent a text message to Steve asking if this was true. But before I received an answer, the deputies took away my cell phone as part of the crime scene evidence. I was cut off from all communications with people other than the police. For the next seven hours I thought Gabby was dead.

I overheard someone else say the guy who looked like Santa Claus had died. I assumed they were talking about Ron Barber. Being under the impression that not only the congresswoman but also her district director had passed away was a very difficult thing.

Steve and Kelly arrived and ran toward me to give me a

hug. As they approached, the authorities said, "*No*. Get away. You're not allowed to touch him." So I asked Kelly to call my parents to let them know where I was.

Kelly and Steve were taken into the hospital with Gabby's mother, Gloria. Later Kelly told me that they stayed in a room with Ron Barber's family. Together they held hands and prayed. When a social worker asked Kelly and Steve how they knew me, she gave a long explanation, and the social worker said, "Oh, you are 'framily,' friends and family."

I remained outside the medical center for what seemed like an eternity. I knew my name badge and clothes were covered in blood, but it didn't matter, because I was waiting for the crime scene investigators to come and either confiscate them or take pictures. They wound up doing both. They took pictures of how much blood I had on my clothes, and how much blood I had on my hands, to have as documented evidence. I needed to go to the bathroom, but they wouldn't let me. Probably they knew I'd wash my hands, and doing that would alter the evidence.

Then the investigators interviewed me in a mobile command unit. Two agents from the Pima County sheriff's office questioned me for about an hour. They were very matter-of-fact, which I appreciated. Each of them had a tape recorder, so if anything happened to one machine, they'd have a backup. They were trying to figure out who I was, why I'd been at the event, what I'd done, who I'd seen. I told them about glimpsing the shooter. I wanted to ask them about Gabby's and Ron Barber's conditions. But they didn't have any information, or if they did, they weren't telling me.

It was during this time that I finally experienced a rush of emotions. For the first time I let the severity of the situation wash over me. I felt useless. All that I had done to try to tend to Gabby had been for nothing. I had done my best, and it just hadn't been good enough. I feared that not only had my work been futile, but that perhaps I should have tried to help Ron. He had been in better condition than Gabby, but now he was also dead. I'd moved on like he had asked me to, to tend to Gabby, and she was dead. At that point I thought that nothing could make me feel better ever again.

When the agents were finished questioning me, they took me to my apartment to get a change of clothes. My roommate Ryan was watching TV coverage of what had happened, and he tried to ask me questions. I said, "I'm not allowed to talk. I'm okay. People were injured. I'll tell you about it later."

The two deputies came into my bedroom and watched as I undressed, to make sure that I didn't leave anything behind that was part of the crime scene. They needed as evidence everything I was wearing, from my name badge to my under-wear, socks, and shoes. I handed each item to them, and they put everything into an evidence bag that they later turned over to the FBI. The FBI still has those things in Quantico, Virginia. The deputies had also set up a crime scene around the entire parking lot for the shopping center, and my car was now part of that crime scene. They told me I wasn't allowed to move my car or get into it.

They drove me back to University Medical Center. Satellite trucks from all the networks—CNN, NBC, ABC, CBS, Fox, Univision—were lined up side by side in a grassy area at the bottom of the hill, below the main entrance to the hospital. Crowds had gathered.

I ran into Patty Valera and Amanda Sapir, who work for the congresswoman's office. They were trying to find out what was going on, who had been injured. Patty was crying and very emotional. Although they were concerned about the constituents who'd been hurt, they didn't know the constituents' names and were asking mostly about the staff. Patty and Amanda had driven to the Safeway before coming to the hospital. "They're telling us that Gabe is alive and Ron is dead," said Amanda. "But we think we saw Gabe's shoes under a white sheet at the scene."

"Yes," I said. "I know for a fact that Gabe passed away. He never made it to the hospital." All of a sudden I realized that people were confusing the two men. "When I left the scene, Ron had been stabilized," I said. "He was still alive when I last saw him." And I told them that Pam Simon had died.

They said, "We just saw her family, and they said she was taken into the operating room."

Later I found out that when the shooting started, Pam

thought the best way to survive was to play dead. And she played dead so well that bystanders and first responders thought she was really gone. It upset me that people, including me, were giving information that was inaccurate. I had done that when I'd mistakenly said that Pam Simon was dead. Saying that made me realize I wasn't as composed and sensible as I thought I was. I had been trying to stay as levelheaded as possible.

I checked myself into the hospital because I had been exposed to blood. Glass had caused little lacerations all over my hands, knees, and legs. Although I had been able to wash my hands after the evidence had been taken, they still had a reddish tint, and there were flecks of blood under my fingernails. It wasn't the blood of one person, Gabby. It was from Ron Barber and Gabe Zimmerman, too. I had done a quick check on both of them with my bare hands.

I had planned to take all of the proper precautions one should take after being involved at the scene of a trauma, but I wanted to get out of the hospital. When you're exposed to blood, you're supposed to obtain an immediate blood screening to see if you've been exposed to any kind of infectious diseases. When I checked into the hospital, the staff wanted to keep me overnight. I wasn't willing to do it. Then they said they had done a history of all the people who had been on the scene whose blood I had touched, and none of them had had infectious diseases. The hospital staff asked me if I would be willing to do blood tests and screenings just to make sure. I decided not to. I wasn't willing to wait. It would have taken too much time. So I just washed my hands thoroughly and got them as clean as possible.

I went to an area that had been set up in the hospital cafeteria for victims, their families, Gabby's friends and colleagues, and federal agents. Victim-witness professionals were there to provide trauma support to anyone who had been injured. People gathered near a TV to watch tributes and get updates. But someone said, "Turn off the television." Families were hearing false news or false promises.

I saw my mom and sisters, but I talked to Gabby's staff first. Not all of them knew what had actually happened. There were questions about who the shooter was, but at this point nobody knew his name. Joni Jones, Gabby's office manager in Tucson, was there, and some of the other folks on Gabby's staff who had flown in from around the country. I needed to give them as much correct information as I had at that moment. I had been there at the shooting, and I could tell them what I had seen. They hugged me and thanked me.

I still didn't know how Gabby was doing. I didn't find out till fifteen minutes later when I talked to her husband, Captain Mark Kelly. He had flown in from Houston, Texas, and I gave him an overview of what had happened. He told me that Gabby had undergone brain surgery and was on her way to the intensive care unit. I was ecstatic. That Gabby was alive and still fighting was good news. She's always been a fighter, whether she was battling for her own life or standing up for the people in southern Arizona. This was one of the many qualities that I had always admired in her. I talked to both Mark's and Gabby's parents. Gabby's mom was crying and said, "Thank you for helping my baby." Gabby's sister, Melissa, was very grateful and thankful. She's a nurse, and when I told her what I had done, she said that had been the right thing to do.

Then I went over to my mom and sisters, Alma and Consuelo, who wanted to talk to me. My mother had been panicked and worried that I had been hurt. By now it was eight or nine o'clock in the evening. C. J. Karamargin, who was Gabby's communications director, pulled me aside and said, "We know it's been a very traumatic day, but we have someone from the *Arizona Republic* who would really like to talk to you." The *Arizona Republic* is the largest paper in our state. C. J. said, "They heard you were the one who helped the congresswoman. They also have a picture that they will be releasing of you walking with the congresswoman on the stretcher to the ambulance. If we do this one interview, you don't ever have to do another. Would you be willing to just sit down?"

I wanted to be left alone. I was exhausted.

Then C. J. said, "Mark Kimble [who was deputy communications director at that time] will sit with you and walk you through the interview. If at any point it's not going well, we will stop you and end it."

We all sat outside in a little patio area. Jaimee Rose did the interview. She asked me how I'd felt, running into the line of fire to help Gabby. I said, "Of course you're afraid. You just kind of have to do what you can." I thought it was important to emphasize the character of the congresswoman especially in that moment—her strength, her fortitude. So I came up with talking points during the interview.

Having worked in politics and dealt with the media, I knew I had to create short but effective sentences about what had happened. But also, and more important, I had to talk about the character of Gabby. Above all else I knew it was necessary to preserve her image as a strong fighter. Image was important to who she was, and I understood that. Later I found out that the original reports of her death had occurred because of my actions to preserve her image. After I had tended to her wound, the employees from inside the Safeway had brought out clean smocks from the meat department. Wanting to maintain a level of dignity, and to give Gabby privacy from bystanders and any cameras, I had covered her so that the only thing visible when people started gawking was her feet.

When the interview ended, C. J. and Mark were surprised at how well I'd been able to do, and how poised I was. Most people would have been very emotional. Not me. I've always been calm, and that trait may have enabled me to handle a horrific crisis.

I was taken back into the trauma debriefing area and told

to get some rest. There was going to be a lot happening in the next few days. A grief counselor from the federal House of Representatives was going to fly in and talk to all of Gabby's staff and interns, everyone who was there that day. I found out that nineteen people had been shot. Six had been killed: Gabe Zimmerman, Judge John Roll, Dorwan Stoddard, Dorothy Morris, and Phyllis Schneck; and Christina-Taylor Green died from a bullet in her chest, on the way to the hospital. The police had arrested Jared Loughner, age twenty-two, at the scene of the shootings and had taken him to the Federal Correctional Institution at Phoenix.

Chapter Four
MEDIA FRENZY

At last my parents drove me home. By the time we got to their house, it was about two thirty in the morning. I tried to relax by listening to music. I was exhausted and needed sleep.

But at four thirty a.m. the phone began to ring. Kelly called and told my parents that a producer for ABC's show *This Week* wanted an interview. The producer had contacted her, since the police had taken my cell phone into evidence. Kelly's husband, Steve, had talked on national TV about what I had done. "I'm on my way," said Kelly to my mom. "Don't open the door for anyone but me. I'll be Daniel's press secretary for the week." Or so she thought. It ended up being for a lot longer than one week.

It would be strictly a volunteer job. Kelly wasn't expecting to get paid. For her it was all about public service. She had worked for years on Capitol Hill, serving top-level U.S. elected officials before joining the Clinton administration, where she worked as Director of Communications for Vice President Gore's National Partnership for Reinventing Government. Her scheduling experience with the press would help her manage me. The *Arizona Republic* story had been released at midnight, and that's when requests for interviews started pouring in.

When Kelly arrived, ABC was already there.

My parents woke me up a few minutes before five. At 5:05 a.m. I was outside my parents' house in the producer's car doing an interview over the phone on live TV with Christiane Amanpour, the anchor of *This Week*. I've always been a fan of Christiane's. She used to be a war correspondent for CNN and spent time in Bosnia. She's brilliant and prepares very meticulously. She asked me about my immediate reactions right after the shooting. I said, "I kind of just shut off all emotion because I knew I wouldn't be any good to anyone if I had a breakdown."

Kelly said that Christiane was wrapping up her show in DC and getting on a plane to Tucson. And at that very moment George Stephanopoulos, the anchor of ABC News, was halfway to Arizona. They both wanted to meet me in person.

"I don't want to do it," I said. I didn't want all this attention.

"We have to," said Kelly.

I knew why. People had been shocked by the shooting. It

was making them feel better to hear what had happened—a truthful, accurate account. There was too much misinformation and wild speculation on TV and in the press. Kelly pushed me hard to accept all the interviews. She wanted to show that a Hispanic man saved the day in a state that has been discriminatory toward Hispanics. She was right.

"Jump in the shower," said Kelly, "and put on some clothes."

I went inside to get ready. A producer from ABC was going to put up my parents, my two younger sisters, and me at the Westward Look resort for a few days so that the media wouldn't invade my family's home. Kelly drove me to my apartment, where I had all of my clothes, to look for a suit and tie. She woke up my roommates, Ryan and Kim, and gave them orders about what to do. One person was to answer e-mail requests, and she sent the other of them shopping, because she didn't like my dress clothes. I like patterns and stripes, but on TV you need simple colors. Kelly thought I should wear only blue Oxford shirts. I had one blue shirt, but she thought I'd need more. So she had my roommates buy a few extra blue dress shirts and a black one for the funerals.

Then Kelly drove me over to the Westward Look resort. There a room had been set up with a camera. Less than two hours later I did a taped interview with George Stephanopoulos for *Good Morning America*. When we were done, Christiane Amanpour walked in and introduced herself.

After that, Kelly hurried me away to University Medical

Center for another interview. She had already scheduled interviews back-to-back. All of the media outlets were staging there. Satellite trucks completely surrounded the grassy area below the main entrance to the hospital. People were bringing candles, flowers, teddy bears, balloons, and get-well cards, and leaving them on the grass. A mariachi band played, and a guitarist strummed and sang.

News outlets from around the world interviewed Daniel in front of University Medical Center.

It was absolute chaos. Producers were yelling at one another. Two or three reporters put microphones in my face. I had to go from one reporter to another. As I was walking to one reporter, Kelly would hand me her phone, and I would do either a print interview for a newspaper or a radio interview over the phone. In between interviews I was doing other interviews. We couldn't move from one satellite truck to another, because people lined up to shake my hand, hug me, and ask for my autograph. We were getting between sixty and ninety calls an hour. Kelly handled managing all the requests. She put her name and cell phone number on my Facebook page. She was scheduling me for five minutes at a time so that I could handle as many of the requests as possible. It was strange and surreal.

I repeated similar responses over and over. Most of the time the interviewers were trying to figure out who I was. I told them what I did with Gabby, but I didn't get into specifics. I didn't give many details. They didn't need to know I had seen Gabe, who was dead by the time I got to him. I kept checking with C. J. at Gabby's office to make sure I was doing the interviews correctly and had the right message.

I had to explain what had happened, what I had done, so the viewers or readers could get a sense of the events. Then I needed to hurry to the next interview.

I didn't know how Gabby was doing. There wasn't any news at that point. I knew she was alive and in the ICU. That was all anyone knew.

Eventually I learned that the shooter, Jared Lee Loughner, had arrived at the Safeway in a taxi. A few weeks before, he had bought a Glock Model 19, 9mm semiautomatic pistol. Earlier on Saturday morning he'd purchased ammunition at a Super Walmart. At 10:10 a.m. he had opened fire and shot Gabby and eighteen others. At 10:15 sheriff's deputies had detained him. On January 9, he was taken into custody by the

FBI. Loughner was charged with killing federal government employees and civilians, attempting to assassinate a member of Congress, and attempting to kill federal employees. He was being held without bail in the Federal Correctional Institution at Phoenix.

There were reporters from all over the world: British, Japanese, Chinese, Australian, Canadian, Belgian, French, German, and Spanish. International interest seemed appropriate, given what had happened. It was big. It was the first time a female sitting member of Congress had been involved in an assassination attempt. And it was probably one of the biggest, if not *the* biggest, mass shootings we'd ever had in Tucson—or in Arizona, in fact.

Foreign reporters asked me not about what had happened but more what I thought was the reason *why* it had happened. But I didn't respond to that question, because I had no knowledge as to why it had happened. And I wasn't going to guess, because in managing messages you don't speculate about what you don't know.

I did almost all of the interviews in English. But Univision, a Spanish-language network based in Miami, was interested in talking to me because I could speak Spanish. I was out of practice because I no longer spoke Spanish with anyone but my mother and grandmother. And I speak Spanish from Mexico, because that's where my mom is from.

Ernesto Portillo Jr., editor of *La Estrella de Tucson*, asked me questions about speaking two languages at home. Later I found out that in the Spanish press they called me *el héroe hispano*, the Hispanic hero.

My brief interviews went on all day, from five a.m. to ten p.m. some nights. There were no breaks. I started losing my voice. I was running around from one interview to another. I was suddenly giving up my normal life and work schedule. I missed being in control of what I was doing. Kelly was in total control, and I had agreed to it. I was too busy to get a new cell phone, and had no way of communicating with any of my friends.

John Wright interviewed me for the Instant Tea section of the *Dallas Voice*, a media source for LGBT [Lesbian, Gay, Bisexual, and Transgender] readers in Texas. When the interview was posted, I learned that the headline read, GAY INTERN CREDITED WITH SAVING GIFFORDS' LIFE.

For the past year I had been a member of the City of Tucson Commission on Gay, Lesbian, Bisexual, and Transgender issues. Wright had asked me to confirm that I am gay, and I did. I had never "come out." It was something that just happened as I was growing up. I wasn't hiding anything. Wright quoted me as saying that Gabby has been "a great ally to the LGBT community."

As a result of the *Dallas Voice* article, I did a longer interview with Chris Johnson from the *Washington Blade*, a leading gay newspaper in Washington, DC. As I started talking to the

Blade, Kelly said, "If you do this interview, you will be 'outed' internationally. Are you ready?"

And I said, "Yes." I was already in the middle of the interview and wasn't going to stop.

When the *Blade* reporter asked me if I thought I should be labeled as a hero, I said, "Using words like 'hero,' I think, is kind of not the appropriate word because although those who did step in and took some action were brave, the real heroes are the people like Congresswoman Giffords . . . and the people who dedicated their lives to public service."

When Johnson asked me if LGBT issues had been one of my priorities, I said I was more interested in public service in general.

After the interview was posted online, people sent in their comments. One woman wrote, "I am wondering why Hernandez's sexual orientation needs to be discussed in this article? Do you report that a heterosexual man saved the day?"

But someone else wrote, "I think his sexual orientation is relevant. Our society needs LGBT role models, especially for young people who are still contending with bullying and discrimination. . . . Perhaps this will help somebody who is struggling with being LGBT by giving them hope or inspiration."

I didn't expect to be a poster boy for all the groups I happen to represent—Hispanics and people in the LGBT community. I never imagined that I would become a role model; this concept seemed foreign to me, because I was so used to not getting any attention. I disliked being in the spotlight, so this made me feel uneasy.

As I told a reporter, whether I'd acted as I had during the shooting because I'm Latino or I'm gay or that I happened to be there on January 8 didn't really matter. I'm not a model Latino or a model member of the LGBT community. The best way I knew to be a role model was by focusing on being the best Daniel Hernandez that I could be.

Daniel on the set with Piers Morgan, discussing the Red Cross
and their efforts to promote Save-A-Life Saturday

Chapter Five
AT THE STATE CAPITOL

By Sunday night, January 9, I had done about thirty-two interviews. That evening, over dinner, Amy Wallace interviewed me for *GQ* magazine at the Westward Look resort. She invited Kelly and my roommate Kim, and my sisters, Alma and Consuelo, to participate to provide extra information about me. Consuelo was nineteen then and a freshman at the University of Arizona. Alma was eighteen and was studying at Pima Community College. Amy asked my sisters if they had expected me to do something so heroic.

Consuelo said, "My brother was always very critical and would think about everything twice before he jumped. It surprises me that my brother went toward danger, but it does not surprise me because he has always been such a caring soul and truly admires Giffords and I am sure without a doubt if my brother were to be in any situation where people were in danger he would not think twice about it."

Then Consuelo told about my phone call home after the shooting. "All of my family was so worried," she said, "and in the back of my mind I was just praying that nothing would happen to my brother. I have always trusted my brother's words, and when he said not to worry over the phone I felt a bit at ease despite everything that was happening."

After dinner Kelly took me to Steve's house. Steve Farley and Kelly Paisley have their own houses. They married a couple of years ago and retained their houses—his in Tucson, hers in Scottsdale. She had scheduled a live interview with a morning show in Spain. So at two a.m. she handed the phone to me, and I was questioned in Castilian Spanish. I tried to speak Mexican Spanish to the reporter, but it was difficult because there were a lot of words they were using that I didn't understand, and there are words in colloquial Spanish in Mexico that are not in the Spanish dialect.

When the interview ended, Kelly and Steve went to sleep. I started trying to get a handle on what was happening. There were thousands of e-mails. The University of Arizona had my e-mail address linked on the university directory, and several of the news outlets had listed my e-mail as well. Many notes came from personal friends who were concerned. I tried to send e-mails to friends all over the state, letting them know what had happened.

But there was one hate mail sent to me and the city council and the mayor of Tucson. The man wrote that it was nice that I had done what I had done, but I was still going to go to hell for being gay. I quickly learned to brush these messages aside.

By five a.m. I was back at UMC in my blue shirt and tie doing another interview with C. J. Karamargin, Gabby's director of communications. Then Steve and I did the *Today* show by satellite feed with Matt Lauer, who was at the site of the shooting. Another day without sleep. I was getting really tired. The more interviews I did, the more Kelly scheduled.

That morning Kelly drove me to the state capitol in Phoenix about two hours away, and Steve took my sisters. We were Steve's guests at the Arizona legislature opening day. He's assistant minority leader. At first Kelly stayed upstairs in Steve's office handling the barrage of phone calls while my sisters and I sat with Steve down on the main floor of the house of representatives. Then Kelly joined us. I was on the aisle next to Steve. When Governor Jan Brewer came in and went to the lectern, she said she had intended to give her State of the State address.

"But not now," she said. "Not today. Tragedy and terror sometimes come from the shadows. . . . That happened on Saturday, when a gunman took away people we love. . . . The gunman gravely wounded others, people we love and respect." She asked for a moment of silent prayer. Then Governor Brewer named the victims who had been killed and wounded, and recognized Arizonans who had helped them. "Daniel Hernandez . . . showed no fear in the face of gunfire," she said. "His quick action in going to Gabby Giffords's aid likely saved her life. Daniel is here today, and I'm going to ask him to stand and receive the thanks of a very grateful state." I stood up, and everyone rose to their feet, clapping. The governor ended her talk with inspiring words. As she walked out of the chamber, she stopped to hug me and pat my back.

Daniel speaking at a press conference in front of the Arizona
state house after being introduced by Governor Brewer

Afterward we met with Governor Brewer, and my sisters and I had our picture taken with her. The Democrats of the state legislature gave a press conference outside the state capitol, and Steve told how I had called him from the ambulance on the way to the hospital with Gabby. And how I had been covered in blood from head to toe when he and Kelly had arrived at UMC. Steve said that on the night of the shooting there had been a candlelight vigil. During the press conference Steve said, "We must make people feel better about what happened. . . . We can, here in Arizona, show the rest of the nation how to govern in a civil manner."

Kelly kept getting press calls, and I did more interviews that day, ending with Rachel Maddow at MSNBC. Kelly said the calls were coming so fast that she couldn't listen to her voice mails without being interrupted. That night we all stayed at her house in Scottsdale, a suburb of Phoenix. Kelly took the phone off the hook so that I could sleep for the first time since Saturday.

Daniel visiting Rachel Maddow in her New York City office

While we were still in Phoenix, she had told me that President Obama was coming to Tucson on Wednesday. Accidentally I ignored two calls from the White House. One of the messages said, "The president is sitting in the Oval Office and would like to speak to Mr. Hernandez in the next half hour." By the time I listened to the message, it was too late to phone back. But luckily I ended up seeing the president in person.

Chapter Six
Tucson Memorial

THE SEMESTER WAS SUPPOSED TO START ON WEDNESDAY, JANUARY 12, but classes were delayed for a day because the president came to the University of Arizona. A memorial ceremony was held at the McKale Center, an athletic stadium mostly used for basketball games. The place was packed. There were a lot of Secret Service people.

Before the program began, my parents and sisters were backstage meeting the president and the First Lady. I stayed in the audience waiting to be seated. Panicked that I might actually have to speak during the program, I had jotted down a few notes. Even at that stage I was thinking that I would be told that my contributions would not be necessary. I still knew my place. I was a twenty-year-old intern and felt like I had no business speaking before an audience of millions on the same program as the president and governor.

As the program was about to start, Gabby's mother, Gloria, came over to me and embraced me in a massive hug that only a mother could give. She was crying and simply said, "Thank you for saving my baby." She then reached toward my neck and asked if I had a chain like the kind she was wearing. I told her I don't like jewelry, and was confused as to why she was asking about jewelry at a time like this. She then took off her chain that had a silver medallion of the Virgin of Guadalupe, a Catholic Mexican religious icon. She said that Gabby had bought the medallion for her when she'd been studying in Chihuahua, Mexico, and had brought it back as a gift. Gloria put it on me and said, "It's a loan. You're not allowed to take it off till Gabby goes back to work." I've had it on since then, and I haven't taken it off. (Although Gabby voted on a piece of legislation in August 2011, she has been in rehab and has not returned to work full-time.)

Gloria Giffords's Virgin of Guadalupe
medallion, which she lent to Daniel

Gloria went back to her seat because the ceremony was about to start. Staff had assigned our places. I was still standing when President Obama approached me. I wanted to shake hands. He came in for a hug and whispered, "Mr. Hernandez, I've heard so much about you. I'm honored to meet you." He asked me questions about what had happened, really briefly. And I told him what had happened, and he said he was very proud. He introduced me to Michelle Obama, and she said the same thing. I talked to her for about thirty seconds. She was very kind and gracious. She also did hugs instead of handshakes. If I don't know someone, I prefer to do a handshake most times, even if it is the president of the United States, but in the last year I've learned to be okay with more people hugging me than I am usually comfortable with. The president sat down next to me. I was between him and Supreme Court Justice Sandra Day O'Connor. She was an Arizona native and one of my personal heroes, having been a leader in Arizona's state capitol for many years before becoming the first female Supreme Court justice. Michelle Obama sat on the other side of the president, and Mark Kelly, Gabby's husband, was next to her.

The program opened with the Tucson Symphony Orchestra playing *Fanfare for the Common Man* by Aaron Copland. Then Dr. Carlos Gonzales, who's on the faculty of UA, gave a traditional Yaqui blessing with a feather. He told how he was half-Mexican and half–Native American, and was from the south side of Tucson, which is where I grew up. He said how great it was that he could get an education at the University of Arizona and come back here and teach.

Next Dr. Robert Shelton, who was president of our school at that time, welcomed everyone to the event, called "Together We Thrive," and then we all sang the national anthem.

When Dr. Shelton spoke, he said, "Tonight we are gathered here as a community to mourn a tragic and senseless loss. . . . No one who lives here was untouched by the events of last Saturday. Over the past few days I have repeatedly heard people ask, 'How could such a thing have happened, and how could it have happened here, in *our* town?' . . . This attack . . . has changed us all." He said that hosting the ceremony would begin "the process of healing." Then he said, "Among the many heroes this week was one of our students." He called my name, and everyone stood and cheered. President Obama turned to me and joined in the applause.

Photo courtesy *Arizona Daily Wildcat*

President Obama applauds Daniel at the Tucson memorial program.

I was terrified, although I tried to appear calm. I knew I was supposed to speak. But I forgot my notes on the chair. As I started to walk to the podium, a staffer whispered to me, "Don't f*** it up."

My friend Emily Fritze, who was then president of the ASUA (Associated Students of the University of Arizona), went up with me and spoke first. She told how she, too, had been an intern on Gabby's staff. "We need to continue to be devoted public servants," she said. Then Emily gestured to me and said that, as a friend, "I was not surprised to hear of his actions of selfless courage. . . . I introduce to you my fellow student and dear friend Daniel Hernandez."

Everyone rose to their feet and applauded again. I faced President and Michelle Obama, and public dignitaries, and a crowd of more than twenty-seven thousand people. Millions more were watching on TV. It was one of the scariest things I ever had to do. But somehow I knew what to say.

"I'd like to . . . start off with a few words," I began. "*E pluribus unum*. . . . Out of many, one. One thing that we have learned from this great tragedy is, we have come together. On Saturday we all became Tucsonans. On Saturday we all became Arizonans. And above all, we all became Americans.

"Despite the horrific actions that were taken on Saturday, where so many were lost," I went on, "we saw glimmers of hope. These glimmers of hope come from people who are the real heroes." I humbly regretted that I was not one of them and named Pam Simon, and Congresswoman Giffords, and Ron Barber, and the first responders, and people like Dr. Rhee, who was doing an amazing job making sure that Gabby was okay and treating the others who had been injured.

Again the crowd gave me a standing ovation.

"We have all come together," I said, "to realize that what defines us is not the differences. . . . We are all a family. We are all Americans. And we must recognize that the real heroes . . . are the people who have dedicated their life to public service." I thanked the audience for their tributes but said, "I must reject the title of hero and reserve it for those who deserve it . . . the people who have made sure that they have dedicated their life to taking care of others."

Daniel being introduced by Emily Fritze at the memorial

There were cheers as I left the podium and returned to my seat. Michelle Obama hugged me again.

Governor Brewer spoke next. "Thank you, Daniel, for your very uncommon courage that likely saved Gabby Giffords's life," she said. Then she thanked the president for coming to help with the healing. As she talked, I sat with my hands clasped in my lap. I didn't know how to react, especially when I was being recognized. I was uncomfortable with praise, because I felt I didn't deserve it.

Following the governor's presentation, Janet Napolitano, the secretary of the Department of Homeland Security, who before joining the Obama administration had been the governor of Arizona, and Eric Holder, the attorney general, each read from the Bible.

Then Dr. Shelton said, "We are truly honored to have the leader of our great nation with us here tonight. . . . Please welcome the president of the United States, Barack Obama."

I stood up along with everyone else, and we all kept applauding. Finally the president asked us to be seated, and he began his speech.

"On Saturday morning Gabby, her staff, and many of her constituents gathered outside a supermarket to exercise their right to peaceful assembly and free speech," he said. "They were fulfilling a central tenet of the democracy envisioned by our founders." He described Gabby's tradition of Congress on Your Corner, and said, "The six people who lost their lives . . . represented what is best in us." One by one, he told a little about each of the victims as if he had known them: Judge Roll, Dot Morris, Dorwan Stoddard, Phyllis Schneck, and Gabe Zimmerman.

"And then there is nine-year-old Christina-Taylor Green," he said in a low voice. "She showed an appreciation for life uncommon for a girl her age. . . . Our hearts are broken by their sudden passing. Our hearts are broken—and yet . . . our hearts are full of hope and thanks for the thirteen Americans who survived the shooting, including the congresswoman."

At that point I had no updates on Gabby. I just knew that Dr. Rhee had performed brain surgery on her and she remained in critical condition at UMC. Then the president uttered the following words:

"I have just come from the University Medical Center . . . where our friend Gabby courageously fights to recover," he went on. "I want to tell you . . . right after we went to visit, a few minutes after we left her room . . . Gabby opened her eyes for the first time."

The crowd roared. I was elated. Michelle Obama squeezed Mark's hand and smiled.

"Gabby opened her eyes," repeated President Obama more loudly, "so I can tell you, she knows we are here, she knows we love her, and she knows that we are rooting for her through what is undoubtedly going to be a difficult journey. . . . Our hearts are full of thanks for that good news, and our hearts are full of gratitude for those who saved others."

Then he said, "We are grateful to Daniel Hernandez, a volunteer in Gabby's office."

"And, Daniel, I'm sorry," continued the president in a mock scolding tone, "you may deny it, but we've decided you *are* a hero, because you ran through the chaos to minister to your boss and tended to her wounds and helped keep her alive."

Everyone rose and applauded. I stood too and took a deep breath. In the next part of his speech the president praised others who had acted heroically on Saturday. Then he talked about how we could honor the fallen by listening more carefully to one another, showing more kindness and compassion, and having "civil discourse." He said of Christina-Taylor Green, "Here was a young girl who was just becoming aware of our democracy. . . . She saw public service as something exciting and hopeful. . . . I want to live up to her expectations. . . . I want America to be as good as she imagined it."

In closing he said, "May God bless and keep those we've lost in restful and eternal peace. May He love and watch over the survivors. And may He bless the United States of America."

He returned to his seat and on his way kissed and hugged his wife, and kissed her again as we all remained standing and applauding. He sat down with his head bowed.

It was one of the best, if not *the* best, speeches President Obama ever gave. I learned later that while I was speaking, people observed him making several edits in his speech because of some of the comments I made. He had a binder for making notes.

Afterward, because of what he said about me, little kids came over and crowded around me. They wanted to know what it was like to sit next to the president, and they asked for my autograph. I stopped to talk to them and was late for an interview with Fox News. But I knew that it was more important to speak to the kids than to do yet another interview. A producer came down to yell at me because we were missing our window for the live interview. I finally made it through the crowd of people wanting to take pictures or say hello.

Outside in the press area, where satellite trucks had parked to cover the president's speech, I did seven more interviews. Reporters repeated the president's words. I felt shy about accepting the title of "hero," but I was beginning to learn how to take the compliments.

Daniel meeting Nancy Pelosi at Together We Thrive

Chapter Seven
After the Tragedy

By Thursday, the day after the memorial ceremony, I had done 215 interviews and I was still receiving nonstop requests to do more. There were calls from all over the globe. My friend and volunteer publicist, Kelly, said the normal press cycle had been extended by the president's visit. She encouraged me to speak to the world. Having to talk about what had happened and go through it and process it out loud, even though it was in public, was actually the way I ended up being able to cope with everything.

The editor of *La Estrella de Tucson* even interviewed my parents and sisters about me. "It's nice to know that people look up to him," said Consuelo. Alma said, "It sometimes makes me mad because he's so calm."

My dad said, "We always tried to impart on him to help his community and do the best he can."

The article ended by reporting that UA students were returning to classes that day but I was not.

Over the phone I spoke to my adviser, Chrissy Lieberman, who said that the university wanted to work with me to find the best course of action, since I had to handle this media frenzy. One possibility was that I could withdraw for the semester. Instead I decided to drop out of all my regular classes except for the internship program. I planned to work for Gabby's office because I felt that my work there was not done. I had much more to do to be of help to the people in the office, but above all I felt a sense of duty to Gabby to continue her work. I increased the hours of the internship from three to twelve so that I would still be a full-time student and receive a certain number of credits for the semester.

On Saturday, exactly a week after the shooting, Christiane Amanpour moderated a town hall meeting at Saint Odilia church, the home parish of Judge Roll and Christina-Taylor Green, who had had her first Communion there. The meeting was televised for ABC News's *This Week*. Christiane called it "After the Tragedy: An American Conversation Continued." She had gathered people from Tucson who'd been there at the scene and at the hospital, the people most closely affected. She did a great job of talking about the roots, getting to the core, without sensationalizing the event.

I sat on the stage with a panel that included those of us who'd been involved that day, and also Representative Debbie Wasserman Schultz from Florida, a close friend of Gabby's. I had never met Representative Wasserman Schultz before. She said to me, "I know you don't like the 'H' word, so I'm just going to call you a mensch." I knew that meant "a good person" in Yiddish. It was at that moment that I remembered better times of working and campaigning for Congresswoman Giffords and Hillary Clinton. I'd picked up Yiddish then because older Jewish women on the campaign would affectionately call me *bubeleh* mensch. I cracked a halfhearted smile, but it was good to think of better times. I was wearing the silver medallion that Gabby's mother had loaned me. I kept it on the outside of my white shirt.

Christiane opened the program by reviewing the events of the previous Saturday and announced that the Safeway market and parking lot were open again and no longer a crime scene. A picture of Jared Lee Loughner appeared for TV audiences. She described him as a man with "a twisted view."

Then she asked the panel, "What is the lasting impression that you will take away from that day?" Turning to me, she said, "You rushed to Congresswoman Giffords as she was lying bleeding, and by all accounts you really set the stage for saving her life. A week later do you think about what it took for you to run towards her even as there was gunfire?"

"No," I said. "I think, really, had it been someone else, I would have done the same thing. Although Gabby is someone whom I've admired for years and I consider a friend, I think at this point anyone would have done the same thing for anyone, because it's a human being and you need to make sure that you help those in need."

Then she questioned Pat Maisch about how she had grabbed the shooter's magazine as he'd been pulling it out of his pants pocket to reload. And Bill Badger told how he had tackled the gunman. He said how quickly we had all bonded as a result of our actions. I had visited Ron Barber in the hospital right after the shooting. Since then we hadn't seen each other that often, but we talked on the phone and sent e-mails to keep tabs on how the other was doing. Later on we were all invited to sit together at various events like Heroes Day when the sheriff of Pima County gave medals to us and officers and first responders.

Dr. Bowman and his wife, Nancy, a nurse, were in the audience, and they talked about their part. "We had just passed Congresswoman Giffords and gone into the produce aisle [of the market]," he said. "Shots rang out very, very quickly.... As I got to the front door, a couple people ran in, one gal screaming, 'They've shot her! They've shot Congresswoman Giffords!' She had blood on herself running into the store." Dr. Bowman and his wife rushed outside. "I . . . stopped behind a pillar," he said, "and there were no more gunshots. . . . The first thing I saw was Daniel with Congresswoman Giffords."

Nancy said, "I came out and immediately started CPR on Judge Roll. . . . A stranger to me steps up and says, 'I can help. Tell me what to do.'"

"Everyone was helping everyone," said Dr. Bowman.

Representative Wasserman Schultz said, "Out of an evil act we have had an opportunity to see the overwhelming goodness that exists in this country."

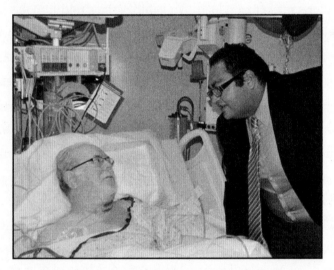

Daniel visiting District Director Ron Barber in the hospital

Christiane asked her how Gabby was doing. And she said, "Better every day. Wednesday was just a miracle to witness . . . [to] have her open her eyes . . . as a result of, we hope, our urging her on to come back to us."

Christiane praised Dr. Bowman and his wife and all of us

as heroes. "Some of these incredible people here saved . . . your friend's life," she said to Representative Wasserman Schultz. The audience applauded. But when Christiane said, "Dr. Bowman, I know that you're not comfortable with the idea of being called a hero," Dr. Bowman said, "I don't think any of us are, including Daniel."

I smiled. "I agree."

In the next part of the meeting, there was a discussion of the ramifications of the shooting. "How can we stop someone with violent tendencies before they strike?" said Christiane.

She asked Deputy Sheriff Richard Kastigar, who was on the panel, how the investigation was progressing. Was the gunman cooperating? The sheriff said that Loughner had been turned over to the FBI eight or nine hours after the shooting and had not given them much information. For the first time I learned something about Loughner.

He had been disruptive in classes at Pima Community College. There had been clues to his mental instability, but the sheriff pointed out that his actions had not been at the level that legally justified arrest. A guy with a dark beard and hair dyed three different colors—purple, pink, and green—stood and said he was a classmate of Loughner's, from poetry class. "In the class that I had with him, he made people uncomfortable, the way he carried himself," said the classmate. "People felt eerie around that, but he didn't *behave* aggressively. [But] you could see a lack of stability."

A neighbor who lived across the street from the Loughners spoke about her observations and said she wished she had had the courage to say something to his parents when she'd noticed Jared Loughner's seemingly antisocial behavior.

This opened up a discussion of mental illness as a chronic condition, and recognizing signs and symptoms, and getting people into treatment.

Then the issue of guns came up, and keeping them out of the hands of the mentally ill. Deputy Sheriff Kastigar said that the person who sold the semiautomatic weapon to Loughner was obligated by law to do so. Christiane repeated the Second Amendment right to bear arms and said this was a very controversial issue. She also noted that, "Arizona is a state which is very fond of their guns." Her colleague David Muir said, "And we could point out that the congresswoman herself, Congresswoman Giffords, was a proud gun owner."

People in the audience commented on gun control. Someone said, "It's time for this country to have a serious conversation."

Although I didn't say it out loud, I don't think gun control was an issue we needed to discuss right then. The issue we needed to focus on was mental health.

In a wrap-up Christiane asked, "How can we learn from this tragedy?"

People talked about the need for more civil discourse. Mayor Bob Walkup said that although he was a Republican and Gabby was a Democrat, they always talked about "what is the right thing for our community."

When it was my turn to speak, I said, "We must be a national community coming together. Something good has to come out of this."

The program was broadcast on Sunday morning. A real American conversation continued. We were sharing what was on our minds, as Gabby had intended.

Chapter Eight
At the White House

On January 23, I got a call from the White House. Brian Bond, the deputy director of Public Engagement who worked on LGBT issues at the White House, extended an invitation to me from President Obama to attend the State of the Union address. I was to sit in the First Lady's box. And I could bring one guest, so I invited my dad to go with me. He had never been to Washington, DC, before. When I called my parents to tell them the news, they were excited but concerned. They wanted to make sure the trip didn't interfere with school, because that was still my main priority. I assured them that I had spoken to my adviser. I wasn't taking regular classes that semester except for the internship program, and those hours were adjustable.

The next day my dad and I flew to Washington and stayed

at a beautiful hotel downtown called the St. Gregory. The manager, Jay Haddock, went out of his way to make me feel welcome, from special attention when I checked in, to nice gifts, including a robe and an embroidered pillow that I still use to this day.

Kelly was already there for an Emerge meeting. Emerge trains Democratic women to run for office, and Kelly was chair of the board of directors for Arizona. She has worked in national and state politics for years and has many friends in Washington. Kelly's friends were able to arrange a private tour of Blair House, the president's guesthouse for visiting heads of state, for my dad and me. Usually it's not open to the public.

The day of the State of the Union address, Tuesday, January 25, was my twenty-first birthday. It was a huge coincidence. In the afternoon I did interviews all over the city. I wore a dark suit, white shirt (my choice that day), and solid blue tie. At ABC News I was interviewed for *Top Line*. Rick Klein, the host, began by wishing me a happy birthday on TV. Then he asked me to describe what it had been like to go through the roller coaster of the past couple of weeks, from being an intern to a national hero. I said it had been a whirlwind speaking before the president in Tucson, and now coming as a guest of the First Lady in her box. I explained that the experience had been absolutely incredible. "I wish it were under different circumstances," I said. "It's definitely been bittersweet." It was still very surreal that this was happening.

Then Rick Klein asked me how I might use my new celebrity. Had I received any job offers? "I've always known that I wanted to go into public service," I said, "and I was inspired by people like Congresswoman Giffords. . . . The events that happened in Tucson on the eighth only reinforced my desire to go into public service." Then the cohost of *Top Line*, Amy Walter, asked if I planned on running for some office in the future. I said I wanted to finish my education at the University of Arizona first. "I'm still only twenty-one, as of a few hours ago," I said, and she laughed.

While I was doing interviews, Kelly's friends took my dad sightseeing. He used to do construction work, but the year before, he'd fallen off a dumpster on a job and shattered his ankle, so he was using crutches. Kelly said it was easier for them to navigate him in a wheelchair because they were doing so much walking.

At six thirty that evening we went to the White House for a reception. It was unreal. I could hardly believe this was happening to me, and felt numb. We walked across the grounds and entered a foyer with Dr. Rhee, the trauma surgeon who had treated Gabby. He and members of Gabby's medical team were also guests from Tucson. And Christina-Taylor Green's parents and her twelve-year-old brother, Dallas, were there. The guests also included Wendell P. Weeks, the chairman and CEO of Corning, Inc., and Staff Sergeant Salvatore Giunta, a Medal of

Honor winner, and it was great to meet these people. Gabby's husband, Mark, had been invited, but he'd stayed at her bedside at the hospital in Houston where she had been moved. Gabby was in the intensive care unit. Her doctors were waiting for her to be ready for transfer to a rehabilitation facility.

Congressional Medal of Honor winner Staff Sergeant Salvatore Giunta
with Daniel at the White House before the State of the Union address

Inside the White House, Michelle Obama hugged Kelly and me. Kelly told her that she had been the state director of the Obama campaign in Arizona and had waited two years to give her that hug. My dad was thrilled to meet Michelle Obama again and to meet Bo Obama, the dog. He's a Portuguese water dog, and we took pictures of us petting him.

Kelly stayed with my dad to watch the speech in the Blue Room, while the rest of us left in a motorcade for the Capitol.

I rode in a van with Dr. Rhee and Ursula Burns, the CEO of Xerox.

At the House of Representatives there was such tight security. A guard escorted us to the First Lady's box. Michelle Obama came in after we did. She sat in the front row next to the Green family, and I sat in a back row.

Down on the floor of the House chamber, many senators and representatives, and Vice President Biden, wore black and white ribbons like mine. In Tucson we had been wearing them since the shooting. The black ribbon was to mourn those who had been killed and injured. The white symbolized hope and peace. The Arizona delegation left one chair on the floor vacant to recognize Gabby's absence. As a further tribute, dozens of Democrats and Republicans crossed the aisle and sat together in a show of support. And among all of the people on the floor, Representative Debbie Wasserman Schultz in her loud voice yelled my name and blew kisses and grabbed others to point me out in the box before the speech began.

When President Obama entered and began his speech, he said, "As we mark this occasion, we're also mindful of the empty chair in this chamber, and we pray for the health of our colleague and our friend Gabby Giffords."

Everyone, including me, rose and applauded.

The president went on to say, "The tragedy in Tucson . . . reminded us that no matter who we are, or where we come from, each of us is a part of something greater, something more consequential than party or political preference. We are part of the American family."

During his speech as he talked about a new era of cooperation and working together, there were frequent bursts of applause and many standing ovations. The State of the Union is a pivotal moment because it is our opportunity to find out where we are and where we will be going as a nation in the coming year. The president touched on many topics: education, public-school reform, health care, the struggle to create new jobs, and shaping the world for peace.

In conclusion he said, "It's because of our people that our future is hopeful, our journey goes forward, and the state of our union is strong."

I stood and joined in the rousing applause.

Afterward we were escorted down to the basement level. I was second in line to get my picture taken with President Obama. While waiting, we got to see people I never thought I'd see in person, from cabinet secretaries such as Hillary Clinton, to the Speaker of the House, John Boehner, who were walking by as they left the Capitol. When I finally got a chance to see the First Couple again, the president noticed that we were both wearing the same tie, and he joked about our "power blue ties." Michelle Obama asked me if my dad and friend [she meant Kelly] were still at the White House waiting for me, and she said that I should tell them it was a pleasure to have had me there for the State of the Union.

Daniel with President and Mrs. Obama

Kelly and I took my dad with us for more press interviews, and then we dropped him off at the hotel. By the time I had finished, it was late. I went to a bar by myself near the hotel to have my first drink as a twenty-one-year-old. It was almost closing time, but the bartender recognized me and gave me a warm beer on the house. I drank half of it. The next morning I got an early call from Kelly asking me how the rest of my evening had gone. I said I had come to the hotel and gone to bed. I neglected to mention that I'd stopped at a bar to have a small drink. But she laughed and said, "I see everything you do," and sent me a link to POLITICO, which had a short snippet on how I had been spotted at a bar in Washington, DC.

It made me realize that everything I did was under scrutiny. I had to be sure of what I did and how it could be perceived.

On Wednesday we returned to Tucson, and my parents threw a belated birthday party for me in the backyard of the home of one of my aunts. My mom baked a cake, and on the top she put the picture of President Obama and me.

Alma, Daniel's parents, Daniel, and Consuelo
celebrate Daniel's twenty-first birthday belatedly.

Part Two

~ GROWING UP ~

Chapter Nine
Life in Tucson

I absolutely love Tucson. No matter what I end up doing, I will always want to live there. To me Tucson is not just a place but is a part of who I am at my core.

I grew up in south Tucson. As a boy I was aware of what part of the city I lived in. My classmates and I were a lot less well-off than kids in other parts of the city. South Tucson is much more working class, low income, and ethnic. A lot of Latino people live there. I can't remember any Anglos in the neighborhood. The only people I can remember who weren't Latino were the African Americans who lived kitty-corner across the street. Our house on South Seventeenth Avenue was small, but I always had my own room.

We were fortunate. My dad was in the construction business and made a decent living during the building boom in

Arizona. My father's name is Daniel Espinoza Hernandez. I'm named after him, but I don't have the exact same name, even though I am considered a "Jr." My mother disliked his middle name and decided to christen me Daniel Hernandez Jr., with no middle name. And on some forms my last name became my middle name.

My father grew up on a farm in Van Nuys, California, a suburb of Los Angeles. He is of Mexican-American descent. His mother abandoned him and his four siblings and left them with their grandparents, who were very strict. He had a tough upbringing. Dad was an avid sportsman, and he played varsity in every sport in high school, from wrestling to baseball. He was recruited to play baseball for a university and major league, but he got injured and wasn't able to play at a higher level. So he and his brother started working in construction and traveled around the country, sending money back for their sisters.

My dad met my mother, Consuelo, at a party. He's ten years older than she is. He spoke only English and she spoke only Spanish, but they hit it off. He was living in Tucson and courted her. She was living in Nogales, Sonora, Mexico, where she was born. There's a Nogales in Sonora, Mexico, and a Nogales in Arizona. The town on the Mexican side is very run-down and decrepit. Very little development has happened in the last thirty years, so the town is not well maintained. I've never liked going there, but Mom enjoys going back because Nogales is her home the way Tucson is mine.

There were thirteen legitimate children in my mother's family. When my grandfather died, we found out that there were other half siblings with families in Mexico. My grandfather had at least twenty children. He made a good living. He owned shipping trucks that brought fruits and vegetables from Mexico to the United States. All thirteen of his legitimate children had the opportunity to study in Mexico. But the women tended to get married, and the men worked in construction. At the time that my mom met my dad, she was working in a lab. They married a year later when she was thirty or thirty-one, and they moved to Tucson. She's now a resident alien. She has a driver's license, but she can't vote.

I was born the year after my parents married, and two years later my sister Consuelo was born, then Alma one year after that. At home we spoke Spanish with my mother and English with my father. My mother and father speak a mix of Spanish sprinkled with English when they talk to each other. Although my mom understands English perfectly, she's not confident about speaking it.

When I was growing up, my parents emphasized the importance of education. While they were still engaged, they discussed their plans for raising children. Dad says he read to me before I was born. When I was little, he read to me every night in English, books like Dr. Seuss's *Green Eggs and Ham*, and P. D. Eastman's *Are You My Mother?* And I'd say, "One more time."

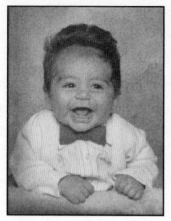

Childhood photos of Daniel and his sisters

But I was always independent. At the age of three I stopped letting my dad read to me, and I wanted to learn how to read on my own. Dad told an interviewer for the *Arizona Republic* that I was *superdotado*, exceptionally smart. "He was scary when he was five or six years old," Dad said. "The things he would come up with. He would just blow us away."

He also told the reporter that at age five I decided to be a doctor like my two uncles in Mexico. This is partly true. Only one of my uncles is a doctor. But I made that decision for another reason.

When I was five, I was on the edge of the bed with my little sisters, Alma and Consuelo. Alma started jumping on the bed, and I fell backward. I ended up opening up the back part of my head. (There's still a dent there.) I started bleeding profusely. It was really a minor laceration, but I didn't think so at the time. In those days we had only one family car, and my dad had taken it to work. So when my mom saw what had happened, she called a taxi and wrapped my head in a towel to control some of the bleeding. We rushed to the hospital.

When we got there, a nurse came up to me, took one look at my head, and said, "It's going to be okay. We just need to clean you up. Everything's going to be fine." She really helped calm me down. Because, when you're five years old and you've only ever heard of people going to the hospital when they're going to die, being there is scary. So they cleaned out my wound and gave me what I think was a CAT scan. Afterward, while the nurse and doctor were waiting for the results, they let me follow them. My mother was hysterical, which is why the doctor took me away. He and the nurse let me shadow them so that I could see what they were doing.

There was someone in the ER who was having a seizure, and I saw the nurse taking care of that person. I also saw the doctor and nurse drawing blood, and trying to handle what was going on with multiple patients. This was the first time I had ever seen a nurse and doctor in action, and I really think that's what started me wanting to help others.

I needed stitches. It hurt, but the doctor ended up giving me five dollars. He told me he was giving me a dollar for every stitch because I didn't cry. Even at that age I was very stoic. I didn't like emotions being displayed. Because of that experience, I was interested in health care when I was growing up. Back then I thought the only way you could help people was by being a nurse or a doctor.

Chapter Ten
Mastering English

I loved going to school. It was a chance to be the best. At Liberty Elementary School I really liked all of my teachers, many of whom are still teaching. I had a teacher named Mrs. Martinez in first grade, and I recently found out that her aunt taught my mother in Nogales, Mexico.

Liberty Elementary is in the Sunnyside Unified School District, a mostly Latino neighborhood. In those days, from second to fourth grade, we had a bilingual program called BIP (bilingual immersion program). Since my mom was from Mexico, I was taking classes in a mixture of Spanish and English. The program helped many of us learn in both languages simultaneously. We were placed in groups and had three teachers who worked as a team: Mr. Wyatt, Mrs. Breckenfeld, and Ms. Rosales. I was a good student, always top of the class.

But in the middle of fourth grade the state law changed and banned bilingual programs. Children could no longer be taught in a mix of languages. Not everybody was Spanish-speaking. There were many Latino children who never spoke Spanish. But those who were not native English speakers, like me, were going to be put into English immersion classes in separate classrooms. Instead of using fourth-grade materials as we had been doing, we would read kindergarten and first-grade books to build up our language skills. We were given 180 days, or the equivalent of an academic year, to "transition" to English. Students who were fluent in English remained at the fourth-grade level.

The way they implemented this was very sudden—sink or swim. It was not a good system. Research later showed that only about 11 percent of those students put into "transition" programs learned English by the end of the 180-day period.

I knew I needed to learn the language right away or be held back at a lower level. I didn't want to be in an ESL (English as a Second Language) class and fall behind.

So over the summer I immersed myself in the English language. I went to the Valencia branch of the Pima County Public Library near my house. It was open every day. Sometimes my mother would drive me, or I'd walk back and forth. I checked out ten books at a time. I went from *The Cat in the Hat* to *The Lion, the Witch and the Wardrobe*. And I read *Star Trek* books because I had started watching the TV show and loved it. I watched anything in English on TV—newscasters, any-body. At night after my parents fell asleep, I watched the BBC News that came on at one or two in the morning, because I was interested in current events. I didn't listen to the radio as much because I liked having visuals.

I completely stopped speaking Spanish at home, although my sisters and parents talked in a mix of Spanish and English. If they talked to me in Spanish, I answered in English. My mother would get frustrated and yell at me for not responding to her in Spanish. She had taken years of English courses, so I knew that she understood what I was saying, but she didn't like to practice her English. My sisters started speaking more in English too. Now, as an adult, I speak to my mother in Spanish, which she prefers, but when I was ten, I needed to learn English fast, so I followed my plan.

My sisters and I didn't get allowances. We asked for things and might get them if we behaved well. Dad felt that he would make sure my sisters and I had whatever we needed for school. "If it has something to do with school, we'll find a way to get it," was his motto. I found out that the *New York Times* had a student discount. I asked my dad for a subscription to the paper, and he had it delivered every day. I got it even though it was intended for college students and I was in elementary school. I really read the paper and for the most part could comprehend everything in it except the finance section.

At Liberty Elementary I stopped talking to some of my classmates because they would speak only in Spanish. As I learned English, I made mistakes and kids mocked me for my thick accent. They would repeat what I said, exaggerating my accent. It made me want to do better than them. I wanted mastery of the language. I could tell I was speaking well when people could understand me without asking what I was saying.

My teachers encouraged me. Most of them were native English speakers, and all spoke pretty much the same way. In Arizona there is no particular regional dialect.

Within six months I got rid of my heavy accent and spoke English well. When I corrected other kids learning English and told them how to pronounce words to help them improve, I was curt and critical. I realize that I didn't go about it in a nurturing way. My teachers wanted me to be nice to the other students, especially those who didn't understand English.

In fourth and fifth grade I had Mrs. Juanita Diggins. I didn't like her at first. She was very stern. She knew that I was intelligent, and she made me push myself harder, even though I was pushing myself as hard as I thought I could. She made me do extra work. I thought the limits I had set for myself were about as high as they could get, but Mrs. Diggins knew I could do more. And if I was talking back in class, which I frequently did, she would punish me and let me know I wasn't acting like I should. We battled. She made me stay after class and miss parts of recess to make sure I was catching up. I felt angry, and complained to my parents all the time. I asked to be switched to another class.

"Dad," I said, "the teacher doesn't like me."

He said, "In life everybody is different. Every teacher will be different. You have to get on their good side."

Finally Mrs. Diggins and I reached an agreement and figured out how to work together. She started giving me ideas of what to read that would be challenging and make me think, but not challenging to the point where I wasn't enjoying it. She had me read the first Harry Potter book when it first came out, before it became a huge sensation. I enjoyed it and since then have read every one of the novels.

My parents were proud of my schoolwork and supported my dream of becoming a doctor. I began researching need-based aid and merit-based financial aid so that I could someday go to college.

When we went to Nogales, Sonora, at Christmas for family gatherings, my mother boasted about my academic achievements. I spoke in English, and my Spanish-speaking cousins thought I was acting snooty. They called me a gringo, a term used by Mexicans to describe white Americans, but in my case the word carried one connotation: smart aleck. Their mothers would say to them, "Why aren't you doing the same as Daniel?" and they would lash out at me. I felt like an outsider in my own extended family, and it grew worse as I got older. I preferred books to sports. I'd bring my homework with me and stay in the back of the house studying. Even my sisters would tease me. My cousins would say, "You're so stupid because you're reading instead of having fun. Oh, that's so gay."

I thought, *Reading doesn't have a sexual preference*, and I wanted to correct the language of my cousins' insults. There wasn't a point when I didn't know I was gay. I was always aware, but at ten and eleven it wasn't that important.

Daniel at about age five

All along I was big, bigger than anyone one else, even in kindergarten and first grade. I was the tallest. Kids my age didn't want to play with me. They'd say, "You're too big." So I'd have to play with older kids or my sisters. They were tomboys and liked to climb trees, but I didn't want to do anything where I thought I might hurt myself. I learned to use my size to intimidate bullies rather than fight. I was always able to come off as someone very big and tough even though I probably wasn't anywhere near as tough as people thought I was.

In fifth grade at Liberty Elementary, I was a hall monitor, and it was my job to stop people from bullying one another or running in the hall. Kids picked on me and called me a sissy, maybe because I had worn a bow tie and vest to school for class pictures (I'd thought it looked "professional"), and because I liked things to be done fairly and equitably.

Once I stopped a boy who was running.

"What are you going to do?" he said.

"Report you."

He shook his fist at me, threatening to fight. I went home and asked my dad how to handle it. "Use your size," he said, and showed me what to do.

The next day I stopped the boy from running. Before he could hit me, I grabbed his arms and put my weight on them. When I let go, he walked away, and that ended it.

One of my teachers, Mr. Wyatt, had a poster outside his classroom about bullying. YOU ARE NOT ALONE, it said. FIND SOMEONE YOU CAN TALK TO. SPEAK UP. COME AND TALK TO ME. I didn't experience too much bullying, but people around me did. The issue stayed with me. I was very angry that we weren't addressing the problems, and they haven't been solved yet.

In fifth grade I wanted to run for student council president.

I asked my parents what they thought about it. "What if I lose? Other kids may be more popular."

Dad said, "You don't go anywhere if you don't try."

So I ran. My sisters campaigned for me and handed out Mexican candies wrapped in paper that said, "Vote Daniel." I wrote a speech and knocked on every classroom door to deliver it.

"Good afternoon, my name is Daniel Hernandez," I said. "I am running for president and I think I will be a great president. Here are the reasons. I am a responsible fifth grade student. I like sports" (which wasn't true) "and reading" (which was true). "I am a peace coach and I am a bilingual student. If I am chosen I assure you together we can make this year fun, exciting, and a different school."

I promised I'd get a new piece of playground equipment for the school yard if I were elected. And I won! A new jungle gym was delivered, and it's still up. Actually it was because of our principal, Mr. Bernie Cohen. He took care of it, but I requested it and had to officially sign off on the use of funds in my position as fifth-grade student council president. This was my first experience with politics, and though I didn't realize it then, it made me eager to do more.

I was interviewed on KUAT, Channel 6, about bilingual classes at Liberty. That was my first television appearance. At the time I was excited about being on TV. Later I realized that I was being used as a pawn. The proponents of the new language program were trying to say, *Look. Everyone can really do well.* But changing the program and eliminating bilingual education was really harmful to a lot of students because it was done overnight. I think the program should have been phased in. It was upon later reflection that I realized that I would use attention from the media only for things that I believed in. I would work for and create my own messages and not be used ever again.

At fifth-grade graduation I gave a speech because I was student council president. I spoke English and Spanish so that everyone could understand. As a present my parents gave me three hundred *Star Trek* paperbacks that they had bought on eBay, and the books are still crammed into a bookshelf in my room at home.

I didn't know then that one day I would be a member of the Sunnyside school board, helping to shape educational policy.

Chapter Eleven
BULLYING

The summer after I graduated from Liberty Elementary, I went to the public library every day and read more than ever before. I stayed in the adult nonfiction section and read every book they had on the holocaust, including Elie Wiesel's *Night*.

Now I get many funny looks when I talk about my deep interest in the holocaust and in all things Jewish. But it goes back to when I was at Liberty. One of the people who taught there came to our class during an anniversary of the liberation of Auschwitz and spoke to us. She told us that her family had been living in Europe during the Second World War and that they'd lived in a country called Hungary. Many of my classmates were too young, and laughed that there was a country named Hungary. I listened intently and learned about the horrible fate that had befallen her family. They'd been imprisoned in their own country and sent off to these places called concentration camps. Most of her family had died.

From that time on I was drawn to stories of people overcoming huge prejudice and obstacles, and never giving up on themselves. I was inspired by stories of people faced with different kinds of adversity, who in the darkest moments found specks of hope and believed things would get better. The belief that they could make things better for others kept them going. And these stories were a great inspiration to me.

In Tucson there were slurs against the Latino community, not so much in our neighborhood and school but in other parts of Tucson. When I went to places like markets and movie theaters in the mall, kids called me "wetback" and "spic," so I knew about prejudice.

The summer before I started middle school, I read books on World War II, and biographies of strong women such as Sojourner Truth, Florence Nightingale, Eleanor Roosevelt, Rosa Parks, and Margaret Thatcher. These women had had to try ten times harder than others to get half as far. They proved they could do things for themselves, driven by what they wanted to achieve rather than what others wanted for them. Sometimes I'd check out twenty books at a time. My parents thought I was missing part of life, and they'd say, "You should have more fun. Go outside and play."

I've never been motivated by fun. Speaking English without

an accent was fun; reading was fun and gave me a feeling of success.

When I started Apollo Middle School at age ten and a half, I was placed in a gifted program, and the number of my Anglo classmates increased. Some of us were doing research, and we went to the University of Arizona library regularly. I enjoyed being on the campus. Sometimes we went there on field trips to the planetarium or the gem and mineral museum in the science center. Even then I knew that I was going to go to the University of Arizona, no matter what.

At Apollo we interacted with kids from other middle schools in events such as spelling bees and honor society competitions. Our teachers told us that the kids from northwest Tucson would be different because of where they lived or their parents' attitudes. The teachers warned us that the kids would be snobbier than we were, and not so nice. I've often found that most people don't live up to whatever description they're given. I don't think there were too many kids who were as bad as they were portrayed by our teachers.

During the years at Apollo, when I was twelve and thirteen, I read *Anne Frank: The Diary of a Young Girl*, and it deeply moved me. That book let me understand what a fourteen-year-old girl was going through, someone roughly my age. Most of my friends have always been girls. I grew up around girls, my sisters and a stay-at-home mom.

My dad spent long hours away at work, leaving early and

coming home late at night. But the economy slumped while I was in middle school, and Dad was out of work for six months. My mom had started baking and decorating cakes as a business when I was in first grade. She was very good at it, and her reputation grew by word of mouth. Sometimes she'd make five or six wedding cakes a night. We would all help. Orders piled in, and my dad and I delivered cakes for weddings, birthdays, and *quinceañera* parties for fifteen-year-old Latina girls. Later, when I started interning for Congresswoman Giffords, my mom baked cakes for Gabby to celebrate every special occasion. Gabby's favorite is lemon cake with lemon filling.

However, I don't like my mother's baking. I don't like cake. I saw too many cakes. Our kitchen always smelled like cake, and bakers' racks stacked with cakes took up all the space. But I admired my mom's success.

We never really ate together as a family. My mother would make something, and then we'd all eat on our own. She had six or seven recipes that she used all the time. She alternated them so that she wasn't doing the same thing every day, but it was the same thing week after week, month after month. I don't like her cooking anyway because it's bland. I like spicy foods.

So at the age of ten, I started trying to cook for myself. I would read cookbooks and watch television to find new recipes. I'd go shopping with my mother and ask her to buy something I had seen on TV and wanted to try. Once, when I was very young, I saw a recipe that had roasted eggplant, and it seemed tasty. But I wasn't content with one eggplant. I persuaded my mom to buy six or seven. She had never eaten an eggplant and didn't cook them properly. It was very mushy and not edible. So I made her buy more and tried cooking it myself. But it came out even worse. When I got older, I kept experimenting and became pretty good at making food. And the more I cooked the more adventurous I became, branching out and trying ethnic recipes from places like Japan and Korea.

My dad wanted me to do normal kinds of things, and for a while I took mariachi lessons, and he pushed me into playing soccer. But the kids made fun of me because I didn't know how to play soccer and I didn't want to learn. They would get on me for not being as good as they were and complain that I wasn't a team player. When we lost a game, the kids blamed me. I was always different from most kids, and I was okay with it. I wasn't very concerned with how others perceived me. I just wanted to be myself.

Daniel and his sisters at a park, after he played a Little League
game for his team, the Colorado Rockies

Looking back now, I realize that in middle school, in addition to the peer pressure to get involved with gang violence and sex, there were different kinds of bullying because people were too fat, too gay, too tall, too smart. I experienced it all. I wasn't surprised that I was a target. All along I had been put down and criticized for working hard and succeeding at school. Kids who didn't do as well academically berated me. At times I began to question whether I should continue trying so hard. If I cut back and put in less effort, maybe I could fit in with my peers and be considered "regular" rather than a gifted smart aleck. At that age there was much more angst and anger than there had been in elementary school because of hormones. Kids were becoming more aware of some of the changes happening to them and to their peers, and acted out.

I knew kids who were straight-A students very early on who didn't like getting picked on for being intelligent. So they went out of their way to start getting mixed up with gang activity because they thought it would show they were tough like their older brothers or sisters or cousins. Instead of being the ones who were being bullied, they started doing the bullying.

We also had kids who were developing eating disorders because they were told they were too chunky or too fat. So they'd stop eating or would overeat and go and purge. We had girls who would dress very sexy because they thought they needed to. Then there were boys who said they had done things with the girls that they hadn't done, so the girls would have a reputation and let that become the truth and live up to it.

When I saw this happening at age thirteen, I wanted to help some of these people, but they needed to want to help themselves. I wasn't going to let anyone else's problems deter me from solving my own. I was trying to accomplish a lot. I had different goals and ideals in mind, and I remained intensely focused on being the best academically to reach these goals.

Chapter Twelve
SUNNYSIDE HIGH SCHOOL

When I started Sunnyside High School, I still wanted to be a doctor because I thought it would be the best way to help people. My sisters planned on going into health care too. In my sophomore year I took advanced science classes in human anatomy and chemistry. I became friends with my teacher, Mrs. Valerie Heller, and she allowed me to participate in Academic Decathlon even though it was for juniors and seniors. There were six or seven of us on the team, and we competed nation-wide on ten different subjects. Since I was already studying two of the topics, science (human anatomy and chemistry) and music (I had an elective in orchestra, playing the violin), Mrs. Heller thought I was qualified. Our team didn't do well, but I enjoyed competing with other kids in academic subjects. I wore a black sweater with the words, "Talk Nerdy to Me," printed in red on the front, and my name in Japanese characters on the back. My sister Alma, who was twelve, borrowed it even though she said our team was like a group of nerds that had formed a club and that the team brought out the dorkiness in me.

"I just wore it to tick him off," she said, looking back. "When he saw me in his sweater, he would get upset and shout, 'Take it off.'

Daniel and his high-school friends, all wearing "I put the STUD in study" T-shirts

"He would tell my mom, and she would tell me to stop wearing it," recalled Alma in an interview. "My sister, Consuelo, and I thought it was hilarious. I just did it to be an annoying little sister." (Alma says she still has the sweater and wears it when it gets cold.)

I would get teased for not going on dates, but I didn't have the time or care enough. I also wasn't interested in girls other than as friends. Kids would say, "You're not doing the normal thing." I didn't listen to what they were saying. I was just going to keep doing what I thought was important.

By junior year I decided that being a certified nursing assistant would be a good way to get ready for a future med school application. I didn't want to be a nurse, but I thought if I had that experience and actually worked with patients, it would give me a leg up on the rest of the kids applying to med school. I knew a teacher, Cathy Monroe, who was a nurse and was giving a class called Nursing Assisting. It was supposed to be for seniors, but she accepted me, since I had already taken senior-level classes. There were about twenty-five or thirty kids in the class, mostly girls.

We learned how to take vital signs like temperatures and blood pressure, and how to properly feed someone, weigh someone, apply a bandage, change a patient's bedpan, change an adult's diaper, and wash our hands in a hospital. I've never been bothered by bodily functions. Ms. Monroe also taught us basic first aid and CPR. We used dummy models like the kind we had for CPR training, and sometimes we practiced taking pulses and blood pressure on one another.

By the second semester I wanted something more challenging. Nursing Assisting wasn't as interesting as I thought it would be, so I started studying phlebotomy on my own.

Phlebotomy is the practice of opening a vein for drawing blood, collecting samples that are used for various tests, and handling the samples properly. I've never been afraid of blood. Cathy Monroe gave me books and other materials, and I trained myself to be a phlebotomist. I learned how to draw blood by reading the books, and I practiced my skills on a fake arm that came in a kit I had sent for. Then I visited different labs around Tucson and asked if I could come in and observe, because I knew I wasn't allowed to touch patients.

During junior year I began participating in HOSA (Health Occupations Students of America), an organization that promotes career opportunities for young people in health care. It's endorsed by the U.S. Department of Education. I entered HOSA competitions statewide, then at the national level. There were many categories to select from, such as CPR/first aid, life support skills, and clinical nursing. One of the reasons I chose to study phlebotomy was that no one else was doing it, and I was almost guaranteed to go from the state competition on to the nationals. And that's what happened. In phlebotomy I was in the top three because there were only two other kids competing.

The Arizona competition was held in a hotel. First we took a reading exam and answered multiple choice questions. If we got a score of 80 percent or more, we could move on to the next level. Next we were tested on the different skills we were learning: drawing blood, correctly labeling the vials, and using the vials in the right order, because some of them have special chemicals, and if you used the same needle, it ruins the test. We didn't draw blood from live people. There were fake pieces of human flesh with varying thicknesses of veins, and each had a bag attached containing white or red fluid. Then we looked at things under microscopes and tried to identify them as bacteria or blood cells. We also had to use a petri dish to grow a culture, so the test was also about lab assisting. I did well, and two months afterward I was a national finalist in the Kaiser Permanente Healthcare Issues Exam at the HOSA conference in Dallas. I went with my teachers, Cathy Monroe and Barbara McDonald, who had helped me prepare. There were about two thousand kids. I did really well and was eleventh in the country.

Now I realize that the stuff I learned there helped me save Gabby's life. I didn't freak out at the sight of blood, and I knew how to stay calm. A few months after the shooting, HOSA honored me at a national student conference for utilizing my skills in a heroic act. My teacher, Cathy Monroe, was honored too. The U.S. surgeon general, Regina Benjamin, presented me with the Heroes Award in front of an audience of about sixty-five hundred high school students. "People look up to you," she said.

"I don't think I'm a hero," I reaffirmed. "It's all the things I learned in HOSA that helped me on January 8."

I told the audience I was grateful for the training I had

received in high school, except that I had ignored one critical piece of advice. "Know that the area is safe before you go into it. I've been getting a lot of flak for it," I said, to wild applause and laughter.

Chapter Thirteen
Graves' Disease

During the first semester of my junior year at high school, I started missing classes. In the morning my dad would wake me up for school, but I'd go right back to sleep. I was sixteen, and he thought I was just lazy and he got upset. He'd tear into me and say, "You'll be late for school. When you were younger, you never had this problem."

But I couldn't help it. Later, when he found out what was wrong with me, he felt bad for having scolded me. I was tired all the time and had no energy. My high-level energy had turned to extreme tiredness. Counselors at school called my parents in for meetings because of my absence and tardiness. They thought I was a truant. This had never happened to me before.

"Dad, I can't figure out what's wrong with me," I said.

At night he stood in my bedroom to check on me and said

my breathing sounded bad. My mom tried to feed me, but over a period of a few months I started losing weight. In one week I lost twenty-five pounds. My parents got very scared and took me to see a doctor. At that time I was covered by a state Medicaid program that provided health care for people at a certain income level, like our family.

At first the doctors told me to cut back on my activities. But when they did blood tests, it became clear that I had extreme hyperthyroidism brought on by Graves' disease. My body was producing too many thyroid hormones and as a result was shutting down. Thyroid hormones affect your metabolism, which was why I had no energy. So the doctors killed my thyroid gland by putting me on radioactive iodine by mouth. I took one pill, iodine 131, which specifically targets and destroys your thyroid. Even after the diagnosis and the beginning of treatment, I remained sick.

By the end of five months, I had lost half my body weight. I got really frail. I lost a lot of muscle mass because I was burning not just fat but muscle. My dad said that it took many months for doctors to figure out the correct dosage of medication. During that period of time I was on a roller coaster. Mostly I just stayed in bed and slept. I didn't have the strength to read or watch TV, not even *Star Trek*. I missed almost the entire year. I didn't want people to come and visit, because I didn't want anyone to see me in that condition. My teachers advised me to drop out of school and come back when I was completely well.

"NO," I said.

I went to school whenever I could, even at the worst of my illness, and somehow I made it to the junior prom. In pictures I look so thin, you wouldn't recognize me. Finally I returned to Sunnyside full-time at the beginning of my senior year, determined not to let the bout with illness slow me down. To catch up and make up what I had missed in order to graduate on time, I attended Weekend Academy. It was a school for kids who had failed and had been kicked out, or who had dropped out, or who had no problems but had chosen to finish school early. We took classes on Friday from six in the evening till nine, on Saturday from eight in the morning till eight at night, and on Sunday from ten till seven. For meals we'd order food from a nearby restaurant and eat together in the classroom and hang out. We all got along and became friends.

Prom night

Meanwhile, at Sunnyside High School, I continued studying nursing and phlebotomy and competing in HOSA events. But around this time, at age seventeen, I began to be more interested in politics as a way of helping people.

I caught the political bug because of Hillary Clinton.

Part Three

~ OBSESSED WITH POLITICS ~

Chapter Fourteen
Campaigning for Clinton

Hillary Clinton has always fascinated me. In 2000 she ran for senator from New York after being the First Lady. I was ten then and in elementary school, but I constantly read about her online and in the *New York Times* and watched reports about her in the news on TV.

When Hillary Clinton decided to run for president in 2007, I thought it was great to have a woman run and possibly win. I liked the idea of a woman president. I was seventeen then and in my senior year of high school. She announced her candidacy on YouTube rather than in a televised newscast from her new home in Chappaqua, New York, which struck me as an interesting choice. I watched eagerly and went to her website.

"I'm in," she'd posted. "And I'm in to win."

I immediately signed up to volunteer in Clinton's campaign.

A few months later I got a call to help with her campaign activities in Tucson. I was really excited. I was getting asked to help because they needed me, something I thought would never happen.

I didn't drive yet, so my mother would drop me off and pick me up. At first Hillary didn't have headquarters in Tucson, so her campaign was being run out of the homes and law offices of passionate supporters. I was one of the only young adult volunteers. The rest were older women, a few men, and a couple of children who were dragged there by their grandparents. I jumped into my internship with both feet and learned all I could about campaign mechanics. My job involved calling people and urging them to vote in the February 5 primary, on Super Tuesday. This meant that a few states were having their primaries on the same day.

At school I urged eighteen-year-old kids to register for the vote. I realized that many of my peers weren't even registered. They thought it was a joke, which was disheartening. I wanted more people, especially young Latinos, to be able to vote and have a say in government.

By then many of the girls I had competed with academically had changed. They no longer duked it out with me to see who got better grades. They were more interested in how they looked and how they dressed and finding a boyfriend. It made me sad for them. Some of the girls were more intelligent than I was, but as they got older, they didn't have role models to look up to. "Caring professions" were expected of them. I thought, *Why be the nurse when you can be the doctor?* I wanted them to have good female role models to learn from, like Hillary.

I talked about Hillary, but she wasn't popular among my classmates. Teenage boys would say she was dumb and didn't know what she was doing. They didn't understand what they were saying and repeated words about health care and the war in Iraq like parrots. They'd put me down all the time.

"You're so gay for helping Hillary," they'd say. "You're so gay for helping a woman."

It didn't have anything to do with a sexual preference. They used the term as a slur, which was completely incorrect. A few girls at school supported other candidates just to spite me. I don't know if anyone actually voted for the other candidates. It was more of a way of picking on me.

Hillary lost the primaries in June 2008 and endorsed Barack Obama. I continued to follow her career with admiration and hoped that someday I'd get to meet her. Twice while I was in high school, I came close. I figured that if I ever did meet her, it would be a quick handshake at a campaign event.

In January 2011, when I went to Washington, DC, for the State of the Union address, I was supposed to meet her, but there was a mix-up, and the plans fell through. But in February when I was in Washington to speak at the League of United Latin American Citizens, my friend Kelly arranged an appointment for me through her friend who works for the State Department. I took my mom along on that trip, and together we went to Secretary Clinton's office on the seventh floor of the State Department and spent an hour with her. I absolutely adored her. She has very caring and nurturing qualities. Secretary Clinton pulled out a chair for my mother and had a huge smile. She had been briefed on the work I had done for her and for Gabby Giffords. With great warmth she turned our meeting into a conversation about me and discussed my opportunities. Before we left, she said to me, "After thirty years I have a piece of advice. Don't let yourself be put into any boxes. Always be the person that defines yourself."

And her words have stayed with me.

Daniel meets one of his heroes for the first time: Hillary Clinton, with Mrs. Hernandez and Daniel in the secretary of state's office.

Chapter Fifteen
Gabby's Intern

After the Hillary campaign ended in June 2008, I realized I wanted to keep working in politics. I'd heard of Congresswoman Gabrielle Giffords and knew of her impressive résumé, but it was not until I met her in person at a campaign event that I became an instant supporter. She had warmth and intelligence, and she inspired me.

I was also impressed that she was the youngest woman ever elected to the Arizona State Senate, and the first Jewish female elected to the House of Representatives from Arizona. So many firsts. She is a strong woman, and I've always been drawn to that quality, but her particular strength was completely new to me. Within days of meeting Gabby I applied for an internship on top of everything else I was doing.

I was eighteen and had completed my junior and senior

years of high school concurrently. In May, I went to the senior prom without a date, just with a big group of friends, and in June, I graduated from Sunnyside High School. I had applied to twelve colleges, including the University of Washington in Seattle, Arizona State University in Phoenix, and two schools in New York City. But my number one choice was the University of Arizona, always, and I was accepted. It's a great school and it's in Tucson, which I didn't want to leave. I had applied everywhere else just to be on the safe side. I planned to start University of Arizona in late August, still thinking I'd go into the field of medicine.

That summer I began working at Tucson Medical Center as a phlebotomist while I was interning for Gabby. The center is one of the largest one-story hospitals in the country and is spread out over one and a half square miles.

I'd work there ten hours a day, then go and volunteer as an intern on Gabby's campaign. She was running for reelection for the House of Representatives. My shifts at the medical center were never consistent. Sometimes I'd be on the first shift, or the second or the third, so I would start work at six in the morning, or one in the afternoon, or ten at night. Afterward I'd go to Gabby's office, which was open pretty late every evening. There was always something that needed to be done for the next day: making copies, shredding lists (she's big on recycling), taking out the trash. But if I showed up in the afternoon or in the morning, then I could help with phone calls and "walking," that is, going door-to-door to get people to vote for her, and to hand out voter information.

At the medical center I was technically an intern, but after two weeks they let me start "doing the sticks." I drew blood from patients even though I wasn't certified, because they thought my training was sufficient. I liked practicing everything I had learned in the classroom. I'd take a little tray of materials to the patients, do different sticks, and then bring the samples back to the lab. I loved working directly with people and talking to them.

I was good and very rarely missed a vein. I had a personal policy against "fishing." Fishing means you stick the needle in and move it around until you find the vein. I didn't like that, because it caused a lot of unnecessary pain for the patients, but there were some nurses and phlebotomists who would do it. What might look like a pretty easy vein might actually be very deep and you'd have to go a lot farther to be able to get the blood.

My colleagues were career phlebotomists in their thirties, forties, fifties, and sixties. When we were working the night shift and didn't have anything to do and got bored, we'd stick one another with needles to practice difficult draws. For instance sometimes people came in who were drug addicts, but because they had blown all their veins, we would have to use the veins on their feet, or on the tops of their hands. There's a vein right above the artery on your wrist, which is a very tricky stick. If you miss, you could puncture the artery and the person could bleed out and die, so we'd practice on one another, and that way we'd be better when we were working with patients.

I didn't receive a regular paycheck for my job. Instead I was given a stipend from a career and technical education program called GO, which is run through Pima County. I was supposed to have been a certified nursing assistant and work on the wards, but I preferred working as a phlebotomist. I was the first high schooler to ever do so. Now they've expanded the program and have two or three interns doing phlebotomy.

I enjoyed my job until it was time to leave in late August and enter the University of Arizona.

Chapter Sixteen
University of Arizona

My first week at the University of Arizona (U of A), I intended to look for ways I could get involved. Gabby had told me that it was important to participate in different activities with people who were passionate about what they were doing. And within my very first ten minutes on campus, I met Erin Hertzog.

She came up to me as I was moving into my dorm and asked if I was registered to vote. I said yes. Erin was surprised. Most of the other students moving in that day were not. She had a full-time staff position with the Arizona Students' Association (ASA), an organization that represents university students throughout the state, and she was trying to register people to vote. I told her about the work I was doing on Gabby's campaign for reelection, and what I had done on Hillary's campaign for the presidency, and she was intrigued.

Erin asked me if I'd be interested in helping to register other university students so that they could vote in the upcoming election. A lot of things were happening in 2008 that were really important. It was a presidential election, and we also had a lot of ballot propositions. Erin said there was going to be a welcoming party for all the new dorm residents the next day and she needed volunteers. I agreed to help.

Erin had been a student body president at the University of Arizona. She was very intelligent and pretty, which helped her recruit young men to register to vote because she caught their attention. We quickly became good friends, and she was to be a constant presence in my life from my first moments at U of A.

I joined ASA, and Erin introduced me to what is one of my biggest passions, fighting for and advocating for higher education and students. ASA works to make sure that higher education in Arizona is affordable and accessible. Only a small percentage of Latino kids go to college. Fewer stay. Once they're there, they fail because they're not prepared, and they leave after the second or third year.

I had applied for financial aid, and grants and scholarships completely covered the costs of my tuition, room, and board. Living on campus away from home was a big change that I enjoyed. For the first time I shared a room, but I hardly ever saw my roommate, Alex. I was rarely in the room, and when I showed up, he was either asleep or playing video games.

My second day on campus I went to the welcoming party on the Mall. U of A has a very pretty campus. There's a lot of greenery and interesting architecture. Our science building is shaped like the head of a cat, and the student union is designed in tribute to the USS *Arizona*, which was sunk in Hawaii during Pearl Harbor. Inside the student union there's a room that has a model of the ship and many photographs and memorabilia. The union also has places for buying food, a bookstore, game rooms, and on the third floor, offices for student activities. I was to spend hundreds of hours crammed into the ASA office, which was the size of a closet, with Erin and other people I really enjoyed being with.

Two of the people I met at the welcoming party are still my good friends: Elma Delic, a girl from Bosnia, and David Martinez III. Elma is a year older than I am. She had been chair of ASA for two years. When I met her, she was involved in a PIRG (Public Interest Research Group). She now works in a public relations firm.

David is a few years older than I am. When we met, he was a student regent for the Arizona Board of Regents, the governing body of Arizona's public universities. In the 1980s ASA had fought for legislation requiring that a student sit on the governing board as the advocate and voice of all the students. David was a senior when he was selected, and it's a two-year commitment, so he stayed on at school and took longer to graduate. Now he works for the St. Mary's Food Bank

Alliance and runs a program called Kids Cafe that feeds low-income and homeless youth all around Phoenix. I see him all the time when I go to Phoenix for events.

As a member of ASA during my first semester at college, I was given a leadership role. I was in charge of the logistics of registering new voters, and I helped train others. We had a lot of work to do. It was a few months before the national election, and the deadline for registering to vote was October 6. Our program was called "U. A. Votes."

Daniel, standing in the back on the left, and Arizona Students' Association colleagues with voter registration forms

Meanwhile I was interning for Gabby on the weekends. I would split my time between trying to get people to vote for her, and working with ASA during the week to register new voters on a nonpartisan basis. It didn't matter who students voted for, as long as they voted.

At a training event I met Emily Fritze, who became another good friend. Later she interned with Gabby because of me. Emily was in a sorority, and her job as Greek life coordinator was to get sororities and fraternities involved in voting. One time a group of us gathered on the Mall in front of Old Main, the oldest building on campus, and we used our bodies like acrobats to form the words "U A VOTES." We wanted to attract attention for our cause, and it worked. From August to October we registered forty-five hundred new voters.

In the weeks before the election, we set up an early polling location and helped people get there. But for many days the effort progressed slowly. People trickled in at a sluggish pace. It was not until the last day of early voting that we were successful in getting a large crowd. On the last day seven hundred people showed up! There were so many voters that we crashed the computers used by the county recorder's office. We had to have a special Saturday of early voting for "emergency" voting for those who hadn't been able to vote the night before.

On Election Day we also worked to get people to their polling places. We had student drivers who volunteered. At one point we had students waiting in line for five hours to vote. I thought it was important to get young people to vote for the first time in the 2008 election. I thought it was more important than going to classes. That was my major mistake my first year.

I was supposed to be a biology major—evolutionary and ecological biology—but I kept procrastinating about taking a science class. And I missed many of the classes that I had signed up for. I didn't go nearly as often as I should have. I thought that in the grand scheme of things skipping one class didn't matter as much as my going and talking to young people about voting for the first time. But it wasn't just one class I skipped. Later, when I got sick again with Graves' disease, it was too hard for me to make up all of the things that I had missed.

On Election Day I was working with "U.A. Votes" all day long to get people out. We reminded students to vote and drove them to their polling places off campus. Some were far away, and we had only a limited number of cars.

The polls closed at seven p.m. in Arizona. By eight o'clock we knew that Barack Obama had won the election and would be our next president. Gabby won too and was reelected to represent the 8th district of Tucson in Congress. She had a great win by a large margin of votes. Her staff invited me to join them at a victory party that was being held at a Marriott hotel near the university. I had also been invited to a small private party for Gabby upstairs in her suite. My mother made a gorgeous cake for Gabby. She decorated it with little icing saguaro cactuses standing beside a replica, in frosting, of a piece of literature we'd handed out to voters that read, GIFFORDS FOR CONGRESS.

Downstairs, at the big party, hundreds of people celebrated and Gabby made a speech for her win. I had brought a few students with me, and they all enjoyed meeting her, even for a couple of minutes, and kept talking about it for weeks.

In my first semester at college, I had met people like me, obsessed with politics. They were the best friends I had ever had.

Chapter Seventeen
Lobbying

Working for ASA was my main interest freshman year. At our meetings I began to learn more about the problems with our education system in Arizona. We got word that there was going to be a 40 percent reduction in state aid for the university, so we organized a protest. I was asked to go to the state capitol in Phoenix. I was only eighteen, I'm Latino, and I wondered, *How am I going to get anything done at the state capitol?* I felt that no one would listen to me, but I went. This was the first time I had lobbied for anything. Lobbying means conducting a campaign to influence legislators to vote a certain way for special interests.

We, the leaders of ASA, got roughly ten thousand students to come from all over the state and protest. Mobilizing ten thousand people is a big deal no matter what group it is. Each of the universities belonging to ASA sent students. At U of A, Erin, David, Emily, Elma, and I signed in people as they boarded the buses. Our slogan was, "Education Should Not Be the Next CasUAlty." The letters *U* and *A* were capitalized to represent our school. We were especially active politically because of the many cuts we'd received. I had often discussed this issue with Gabby. She had been in the state legislature and knew how poorly public education was funded in Arizona as well as nationally.

ASA directors (from left to right): Daniel, Emily Fritze, Dan Fitzgibbon, Elma Delic

At the protest ASA members carried banners printed with our slogan, and we marched in front of the house of representatives. I took pictures of the huge crowd on the capitol lawn. Our demonstration succeeded. As a result the state did *not* cut aid to the university. I realized how effective we could be as a group influencing legislation, and as individuals getting involved in public life.

Through the work I did at ASA, I became good friends with David Martinez. Eventually I learned that he was gay too. David was on the City of Tucson Commission on Gay, Lesbian, Bisexual, and Transgender Issues, representing students. I became much more aware of students' problems. I also realized that the LGBT community oftentimes got put into one big monolith, the way Latinos or young people are lumped together. This was not always useful. Every group has different needs and priorities. Not seeing the needs of young LGBT people being addressed concerned me.

One situation involved a young man, from a religious family in a rural community, who had come to U of A in Tucson. He had always known he was gay but had never acknowledged it to his family. At a party he was making out with another boy, and a relative, who was also there, saw them kissing. The relative called the student's parents and outed him. The boy's family said to their son, "If this is true, we will not be able to help you anymore." The student admitted it was true and that he had kissed another boy, so his parents cut off all financial support for his tuition. "You're no longer part of this family," they said. "You can come back if you're not gay." The student was in turmoil and tried to commit suicide by taking a lot of pills. He botched his suicide attempt and wound up in the emergency room and had his stomach pumped. But his parents would not come to Tucson to see him. I wanted to help. However, his problems were more severe than I could handle alone. He knew, though, that he could count on me for support, and I pointed him to organizations that worked to help young LGBT people get social services, such as Wingspan, an LGBT advocacy center in Tucson.

The incident stayed with me and later inspired me when I was asked to serve on the city LGBT commission. I was beginning to learn that we needed people to be advocates, the voices of students in crisis over sexual identity. Young people had to know of resources available to them.

I didn't socialize or go on dates. I mostly spent time with people associated with ASA. But in the spring I began to miss many ASA meetings and made it only to the important ones. I skipped classes, too. My energy level dropped drastically, and I was too tired and weak to get out of bed. My old symptoms of Graves' disease returned because I didn't have checkups, blood work, or medication. I was not producing any thyroid hormones, and this badly affected my metabolism. I needed to get tests done to see what medication dosage I should be on, but as a nineteen-year-old student I had lost my health insurance. The Medicaid resources that had been available to me at age seventeen no longer applied. The economy had crashed and the state had cut off medical aid for college and university students. Without the medication I needed I received poor grades and suffered academically. I went into bad standing and was put on probation.

My roommate, Alex, had left halfway through the first semester, so he wasn't around to help me. But I wouldn't have asked him anyway. One of the hardest things for me to do is admit that I need help. I felt ashamed and tried to hide my illness even from my good friends like Erin, Emily, and David.

Finally, because of my poor attendance, I was disqualified from the College of Science. I was told that in order not to be disqualified from the University of Arizona, I would have to attend a community college for twenty-four units, or what is typically a full academic year.

I had no choice but to leave U of A and move back home. Over several months I had to prove that I was a dependent of my parents and therefore eligible to receive health care and medication. The paperwork kept getting lost and mixed up, and mistakes were made. At last, toward the end of summer, it was straightened out and I saw a doctor who did tests. I had gone from hyperthyroidism and producing too many thyroid hormones to hypothyroidism, or producing too few. Now I experienced weight gain along with lethargy. A few days after seeing the test results, the doctor adjusted my medication, and within a week or so I was feeling a lot better.

I dedicated myself to overcoming my latest obstacle and making up college credits so that I could return to U of A as quickly as possible. I was already enrolled in Pima Community College because of the classes I had taken at high school in a special program. During the summer I took one class online, the most I could handle.

Out of shame for what I felt was a personal failing, I kept all of this a secret from my friends.

Chapter Eighteen
HOUSE BILL 2668

While I was living at home, I stayed in touch with Erin and David and a few other friends by e-mail and phone. I didn't invite them over to visit me. I've never wanted to mix parents and roommates and friends. Very rarely do any of them interact with one another. I compartmentalize everything.

Once in a while, when I felt up to it, I attended ASA meetings. It was very stressful to not have the energy to do things I wanted. Although I wasn't picked as a director of ASA, Erin created a position for me as senior fellow. That summer she asked me and a couple of other members to research and draft legislation related to students and higher education. We could each choose our own project. I jumped at the chance to be more deeply involved with advocacy for education and to learn how to lobby.

I began researching my topic by looking up information on the computer and making phone calls to groups around the country that had worked on similar legislation. My bill was aimed at getting more students to register to vote in state and national elections. The bill, if passed, would make it legal for university students over the age of eighteen to be excused from class to vote for the same amount of time, about three hours, as full-time employees in the state of Arizona. I felt that this was a way for students to make a difference and have their voices heard. Before this, students were not legally allowed to miss classes for the purpose of voting.

In the fall, as I developed the bill, I took nineteen units at Pima Community College to fulfill some of my college requirements and regain my standing. In one semester I made up a year's credits. By the second semester of what was my sophomore year, the U of A accepted me back, but it was too late to start classes. So for six months I had a break and focused entirely on ASA and working on my piece of legislation.

First I had to find someone who would sponsor my bill. Erin and I went to Phoenix and approached everybody who might be willing. We did research on all the legislators and met with people in the house of representatives and in the senate. Republican or Democrat, it didn't matter—the first one who agreed would sponsor the bill. Sometimes Erin trusted me to go alone. I was good at coming up with convincing points on my own. I presented a couple of pages stating what

I wanted. But no one wanted to work with us.

Finally we met with Dr. Matt Heinz, a Democrat and young physician, who is also a member of the Arizona house of representatives from Tucson. Later I found out that Dr. Heinz is openly gay and one of four LGBT members of the Arizona state legislature. Coincidentally he practices at Tucson Medical Center, where I had interned as a phlebotomist. At our first meeting Dr. Heinz agreed to sponsor the bill and immediately opened up a bill folder. This meant that he sent the bill to people in the Arizona Legislative Council who drafted the wording and made changes and amendments. My piece of legislation was assigned a number, House Bill 2668.

Months passed by before we heard anything more about it. Then the bill came up several times for a vote in the legislature. Erin, Elma, and a few other friends and I drove to Phoenix and lobbied people so that they would pass my bill and others we were working on at the same time. We talked to legislators in their offices or stopped them as they were walking across the lawn in front of the capitol. Although we mainly targeted Republicans because they would be less likely to vote for our bill, I once spoke to Steve Farley, a Democratic state representative from District 28 in Tucson. I didn't know it then, but I was to wind up working for Steve and he would become a close friend.

The bill I had drafted died several times when it came up in the senate and the house. Republicans wanted to make sure that liberals weren't recruiting more liberals to vote. After meeting for one hundred days, the legislature was trying to end the session. We worked hard making calls to get the Speaker of the house to put it on the agenda along with three of our other bills, and we enlisted many students to help us. Finally on the last day of the session, House Bill 2668 came up for a vote. I was present when it was passed in both legislative chambers at the state capitol. Then the bill was signed by the governor.

But there was no time for us to celebrate. We still had many other important things to accomplish.

Chapter Nineteen
CAMPAIGN MANAGER

In late May 2009, I returned to U of A and moved into an apartment off campus. I was nineteen and so glad to be living with people my own age again. My new roommates were Kim Osesky and Ryan Sonnenberg.

Kim and I were already good friends. We had lived in the same residence hall freshman year, and we had both been involved in the Hall Council. Kim was really energetic, which is nice. She was a chemistry major planning on a career as a forensic scientist. She had absolutely no interest or involvement in politics, which was great, because I spent 95 percent of my time with people who were at least as obsessed with politics as I was, if not more. If I dragged her to an event, she said that I ignored her because I was being nice to all the other people I had to be nice to. I could talk to her for thirty minutes about something, and she'd have a glazed-over expression because she didn't know what I was talking about and didn't care.

Kim and I had planned on sharing an apartment, just the two of us, but we couldn't find a two-bedroom place. Ryan, a friend of ours from freshman year, found a four-bedroom and became part of the package. Ryan was usually in bed by nine, and I was never home before eleven or midnight because of all the things I was doing. I had no idea what his major was. The only times we saw him was when he was playing one of his Xbox games, so it was perfect.

We three didn't get along well when it came to dividing chores, so things never got done. I did the cooking, but I never did cleanup. I left it to the others to do it or not. And they didn't.

At the university I resumed taking classes. Around this time I decided to change my major from biology to political science. I just wasn't as passionate about science as I had once been, and I didn't think it was a good idea to keep doing something I didn't want to do. I still had never taken a science class at U of A and only took one senior year to fulfill a requirement. I just really enjoyed advocacy. That means writing and speaking to influence legislation on political and social issues. With ASA I was doing work on issues like public education to make changes in the state of Arizona.

I knew I no longer wanted to pursue a career in health care. For me public service was a better way of helping people. My parents were kind of surprised by my decision. I had always been so committed to the idea of being a doctor. They didn't understand politics and how things work and why student advocacy involves anywhere from eighty to one hundred hours a week of hard work. They were puzzled but supportive.

Toward the end of summer I bought my first car, a used Mitsubishi. It was a small white sedan, nothing special, just a way to get around. My friends and I christened the car Nicki Mirage, a play on the name of a singer we all liked named Nicki Minaj. It was nice to finally have the ability to move on my own without asking people, including my mom, to give me rides. I don't like asking people for anything.

I hadn't learned how to drive till I was eighteen. I had my permit but not a license. My dad had tried to teach me, but now I needed to practice for a month or two before taking my driver's test. So I owned a car before I had my license. I'm very stubborn and was afraid of failing the test. Everything I do is driven (no pun intended) by the fear of failure. A paralyzing fear. I strive for perfection.

I passed the test and needed the car more than ever when I started working for Steve Farley. At that time he was running for reelection as state representative from District 28 of Tucson. Steve had asked my friend David Martinez to manage his campaign, but David said it wasn't his thing. He told Steve he had someone in mind and suggested me. David asked me if I'd be interested, and I was. It was early January 2010, a couple of weeks before my twentieth birthday.

I sent Steve my résumé and then went for an interview at his house. Steve and Kelly live in a "historic property" that was built in 1946. The front door is painted purple, the windows are trimmed in apple green, and there are turquoise metal garden chairs in the front yard near the cactus.

Steve's a public artist who invented a process of converting photographs to glazed ceramic tile. He created a mural at the Broadway underpass in downtown Tucson that honors community history. I'd seen it dozens of times. You can't miss it. The mural features four thousand square feet of larger-than-life historic photos of Tucsonans, transferred onto tiles.

But Steve is also a dedicated legislator. He got involved in politics because of transportation issues. He started a project to revitalize downtown Tucson by bringing in a modern streetcar that goes along a four-mile route. Steve said, "Many people won't even consider riding a bus, but they'll ride the streetcar because it's fun."

I liked his ideas. Once before I had met Steve at a coffee shop near his house when I was lobbying to discuss university issues. Steve believed that all students should be able to afford to go to college, no matter how little money their family has.

At the interview he and Kelly asked me questions as we sat in their living room. I wasn't nervous. I talked about what the upcoming race involved and what I thought I could bring to the table. I understood that Steve was running against four other people and needed to win the primary in August. He couldn't be in Tucson full-time until the legislative session was over. Legislators usually try to finish the session in one hundred days, which means going back and forth to Phoenix. Sometimes they stay longer when the governor calls a special session to discuss a specific issue. Steve needed someone, like me, to go to all the meetings for different Democratic groups in Tucson and be the voice of his campaign, and to let them know what he was working on at the capitol.

Right at the interview Steve hired me. He was shocked at my age and had thought I was older. But he took a chance on a nineteen-year-old and trusted me to manage his campaign and represent him at events. Later he said that he was impressed with me because I was intelligent, earnest, and in command of the issues.

"When you find the right person with the right ability," said Steve, "it doesn't matter how old they are. It was obvious from the beginning that this was the guy. It seemed less like an interview and more like the first day of work."

I was very pleased that I got the job, and was excited that I would have a new challenge. I was to receive a small salary and begin immediately.

CHAPTER TWENTY
LGBT

FROM JANUARY ON I DIVIDED MY TIME BETWEEN SCHOOL, ASA, and running Steve's campaign. Somehow I got enough homework done to pass. I turned in papers late and asked teachers to work with my schedule. Although I was mostly taking classes in my major, political science, I didn't receive credit for doing actual work in the field. I had to do regular assignments like everybody else. But I'm antsy if I'm not doing five things at once.

Steve didn't have an office in Tucson, so we used the back room of his house, which was stocked with computers, phones, and files. My main job was recruiting volunteers, since there was no money for a paid staff. My sister Consuelo wasn't interested, but I dragged my youngest sister, Alma, with me because I needed extra help. In December, Alma had graduated from high school early at age sixteen, and she was taking some classes at Pima Community College, so she had time. She wound up doing the same things I did and got wrapped up in politics, like me. Steve was shocked at how young Alma was—too young to even vote for him—but she enjoyed being part of the team and going door-to-door to ask voters for support.

Before a press conference (from left to right): Kelly Paisley, David Gass, Steve Farley, Daniel, Dana Marie Kennedy, and Katie Hobbs

Walking is the biggest part of a campaign. Steve always said that I was a "relentless walker." First we had to knock on people's doors and ask them to sign a statement certifying that Steve Farley would represent them and should be on the ballot. Every candidate has to collect three hundred to four hundred of these signatures and send them to the secretary of state in Arizona in order to get on the ballot. (The number changes every year, depending on how many people are registered in each district.) We collected eight or nine hundred names.

Before we set out, we would gather at Steve's house and, over coffee and bagels, discuss how we'd approach people. I had a map showing where voters in Steve's precinct lived. We generally have a policy that people never go on their own. Everyone was supposed to go walking door-to-door in pairs. Although we can't control everything, we can try to be careful about volunteers' safety. Sometimes when we knocked, people would come to the door naked, or smoking weed. Alma said that occasionally men came to the door in their underwear or wrapped in towels and said inappropriate things. She thought it was "pretty funny," even when a dog almost attacked her.

Once a guy chased me in his golf cart. Another guy screamed, "Get the hell off my property," so I left very quickly. That's why we usually go in groups and carry cell phones. I always told the volunteers, "If you don't feel safe, don't walk it."

I didn't listen to the rules, though, because other people slowed me down and I preferred to go alone. I still do. But sometimes I worked with another person, and at those times, if I needed help, I relied on the other person to run interference. It's called "staffing."

For example, if I'm talking to someone and it's going on too long, Alma, or whoever I'm with at the time, interrupts and says, "Oh, we're so glad to talk to you, but actually Daniel is running late for another appointment." Or, "It's a pleasure meeting you, but we have to run to the next house." I can't ever be curt with anybody. The voters have to think I'm being friendly and nice, because I'm trying to convince them to vote for my candidate, and Alma is the one cutting it short. Since the shooting on January 8, people often recognize me when we're walking door-to-door, and they want to talk for twenty to thirty minutes. I have to meet my numbers to be effective, so Alma hurries up the conversation. If I'm by myself, I say, "I have to get going."

Sometimes Alma and I would drive to a neighborhood and she'd knock on doors while I stayed in the car making phone calls, to use our time most efficiently.

Walking continues throughout the campaign, right up till Election Day. Part of the job is getting out the word about what the candidate stands for and hopes to accomplish, and asking people to vote for him. For instance Steve was the first legislator in the country to introduce a ban on texting while driving. It failed to get support in the legislature, and he's been pushing the bill for years. He was also concerned with immigration issues and improving educational opportunities, and he still is. Public transportation is another one of his priorities—getting funding for roads, bridges, and trains.

I worked out of my car 95 percent of the time, traveling to different things. I needed to go to a lot of events all over Tucson on Steve's behalf, and talk about the different candidates.

As I worked for Steve, I also helped with Gabby's campaign for reelection. We coordinated things with her campaign office, and she'd send us things that she needed done.

Steve and Gabby shared many of the same ideas and values. They both wanted better funding for education, immigration reforms, and equal pay for equal work for women. So when I knocked on doors to get people to support Steve, I convinced them to vote for Gabby as well. Steve and Gabby had known each other for a long time, and he had designed her campaign logo, "Giffords for Congress."

At events she'd always make her way over to me to say hello. Once she brought Senator Mark Udall to a fund-raiser to help boost her campaign and couldn't come over to greet me. But the next morning, when she was back in Washington, DC, she sent me an e-mail apologizing and asked, "How's school? How's your mother doing?"

Daniel and Gabby with cake that Daniel's mother baked

For Steve's campaign he made most of the calls himself asking for donations. But we had a few house parties when people let us use their homes and provided drinks and snacks. Alma greeted guests at the front door, and I took charge while Steve gave a stump speech and answered questions. Afterward we'd all help with the cleanup. My mom made lots of cakes, and pretty soon our families became close.

Steve has two daughters from a previous marriage, GiGi and Amelia, and they would hang out with us for fun even though they were too young to take part in our activities. Alma says she thinks of Steve as a second father and of Kelly as a second mother.

My parents grew interested in politics because of me, and they'd come to big events for Steve. Before the primary my dad helped make phone calls for both Steve and Gabby when I brought home a stack of names and numbers. I'd write a script for him to follow, but I changed it constantly as issues came up.

I was too busy with everything else to be involved with LGBT groups on campus. Then my friend David Martinez asked me to apply for the job of City of Tucson commissioner on LGBT issues. He was the commissioner then and was leaving for a new job in Phoenix. They didn't have anyone on the commission except David to be a liaison with students at the university. I applied for the position, and David recommended me.

In June 2010, I received an official letter at my parents' home appointing me to the City of Tucson commission on

LGBT issues. At age twenty I was the youngest commissioner they had ever chosen. The mayor had appointed me to be one of his ten advisers. Most of the other members of the commission were in their fifties, sixties, or seventies.

I wasn't at the house when the letter arrived, and my parents opened it and read it to me over the phone. Then my mother said in Spanish, "Don't you have to be gay to be part of the commission?"

I said, "Probably." Then I said, "I have to get going."

I had never formally come out to them. Their finding out was something that just happened. A few months later, after my appointment to the commission, my mom and dad talked with me about it, and sometimes they accompanied me to LGBT events.

As commissioner I now became more involved with LGBT students on campus. My job was to do outreach to kids and make them aware of what resources were available to them for mental health, bullying, and health issues like HIV testing. Wingspan, for instance, provides information and referral services. I wanted to be a contact between young students and the city, and meet the needs of gay youth, ages sixteen to twenty-four.

I'd hear of problems and try to find ways of interacting. Lots of cases involved Hispanics. A person would come out and not have any family support and end up on the street, or get involved with prostitution, alcohol, and drugs. So we had programs to help people who'd been disowned by their families find a place to live. I saw some of my peers going through this.

I was also an advocate of students' rights to have affordable college tuition. Prior to my appointment as commissioner, I knew someone in great need. He was gay, and studying engineering at U of A. He had saved up money for school, and his mother, a single parent, helped him. Then his mother got ill and could no longer work. Before, because of his mother's income, he hadn't qualified for financial aid. Now, based on the previous year's taxes, he didn't qualify for aid, and he couldn't ask his mother for support, yet he needed to continue his education. He tried paying his tuition himself and for four months lived out of his car in the campus garage and showered at the gym. He spent time in the student union or the library and didn't leave the university. He ate only twice a day at Burger King, ordering from the ninety-nine-cent menu. I met him once going into classrooms, and I gave him my e-mail address and cell phone number. But after a while he couldn't keep it up and go to school, and he started working at a restaurant. It was heartbreaking. His story was one of many like it, and made me more aware of different things going on.

I was trying to be the voice of people in turmoil. Many don't have the capability to speak for themselves. However, my job as commissioner wasn't as proactive as I thought it would be. I wanted more of an advocacy role than I had. Instead I mainly went to monthly meetings, where the issues discussed didn't have anything to do with my priorities—students. The commission would talk about community businesses and give reports on how little was getting done rather than discussing the needs of students.

Meanwhile, I continued campaigning for Steve and Gabby throughout the early summer. Steve said, "You know, walking door-to-door in Tucson in July is not an easy thing to do." It gets hot, about one hundred degrees every day. But we did it. The primary was held in August, and Steve won. My mom made him a victory cake (his favorite, like Gabby's, lemon with lemon custard filling) to celebrate. But once Steve won, he didn't need to keep his campaign running as hard, because the district was safe. They had chosen him in the primary and would most likely vote for him in November. So he encouraged me to do some work in a different part of Tucson.

Chapter Twenty-one
Knocking on Doors

I was technically still Steve's campaign manager, but he asked me to help his colleagues in a more difficult district. Two women were running for the state legislature in District 26 in northwest Tucson. "They need your help more than I do," he said. Nancy Young Wright was an incumbent, and Cheryl Cage was running for the second time in a district that didn't favor Democrats.

District 26 was within Gabby's congressional District 8, so I was helping her as well. She wasn't ahead in the polls and risked losing her seat. District 8 is a conservative area, predominantly Republican, less concerned with issues such as immigration reform, health care, and minimum wage. So it was important to get Democrats out to vote for Gabby, Nancy, and Cheryl. My job was to do what I had done for Steve: go door-to-door canvassing and try to get voter support.

People are prone to say rude things when you're canvassing. They make threats because you are coming into their space. I had guns pulled on me twice. One person had a sign on his front lawn that read, I HAVE THE SECOND AMENDMENT RIGHT AND I'M NOT AFRAID TO USE IT. He came to the door, and as I started speaking to try to find out if he was a supporter or an opponent, he pulled out a gun from his back pocket and just began playing with it. I don't know much about guns, but I could see that it was a revolver. I wasn't afraid. I doubted anyone would be shooting for no reason. He was likely to be an opponent, considering how extreme they are about the Second Amendment, but my mission was to get as many people to talk to me as possible, regardless of their position. As I talked, he stroked the shaft of the gun, playing with it in a very threatening manner, trying to show me who was the dominant one in the conversation. But I was not going to be intimidated by anyone, so as he kept playing with the gun, I kept asking questions.

"Are you familiar with the candidates, Gabby, Nancy, and Cheryl?" I asked.

If he said yes and that he was leaning toward them, then I'd say, "Thanks for giving me your time." But if not I'd use talking points about the candidates and give him handouts for each of them. It turned out he really liked Gabby, but he didn't want to support the other two people who were running. He said he appreciated that I had taken the time to talk to him.

The conversation had lasted five minutes. At the end he said, "I'll be supporting the congresswoman even though I don't agree with her on everything. But she's doing a good job and she's doing her best."

In rural parts of southern Arizona, ranchers routinely come to the door wearing guns in holsters on their waists. It's much more common out there. One time a guy came to the door rubbing one side of his hip where he had his gun. He made eye contact with me and said, "Get off my property." He pointed to signs in front of his house saying NO TRESPASSING and NO SOLICITING. But I wasn't soliciting. I had a mission and stayed calm. I was knocking on doors for Gabby.

The man said, "I have a gun, and I'm not afraid to use it. I know *how* to use it."

I stayed focused. I had work to do. This was a race where we needed those people who were Independents or Republicans. We had to talk to voters who were on the fence and still undecided. Finally I thanked him for his time and moved on. I was not going to get down to his level.

Another time a homeless man chased me while I was walking house to house. He came toward me in a threatening manner. I ran toward my car at the end of the street and outran him. But I still had another fifty houses to canvass. I got in my car and drove three streets away and finished walking to the houses on my list.

Of course my parents worried about my safety. I never

told them about some of these incidents and how often I went door-to-door. They knew the job had to get done. Knocking on doors can be much more effective than sending mail. My parents supported Gabby and Steve and attended events that involved me.

I invited them to a debate among Gabby; Jesse Kelly, a Republican member of the Tea Party; and former state senator Jonathan Paton, also a Republican. The two Republicans were running against Gabby for her House seat. I did that event for ASA, which is nonpartisan. I didn't want people in the Jesse Kelly campaign to be upset because I was working for ASA but was obviously a little biased. So I mostly worked backstage on logistics. I had told my parents to be there at a certain time so that I could come out and escort them into the ballroom to guarantee their seating for the debate. But they were late, so I couldn't take them to their seats. When they arrived, my dad was in his wheelchair because he was still suffering from his shattered ankle and had problems with his leg, so they went on the elevator. I later found out that in the elevator they ran into another man who was also in a wheelchair, who happened to be Gabby's father. My parents hadn't met him before, but when they were riding up in the elevator, they started talking and ended up sitting together for the entire debate. And Gabby's father kept asking my parents questions about how they thought Gabby was doing, and my dad told him about how much they liked her and how I had been working on her campaign. At the end Gabby's father said, "Oh, by the way, I'm Spencer. I've met your son. I'm Gabby's dad."

A few days before the election I ran into Gabby, her husband, and her parents at a block party she was holding at the Hotel Congress, one of her large supporters. I helped staff the event. They had a lot of live music and guest DJs, including Steve. I brought Alma with me, and she wanted to go out to grab some food. As we were leaving, Gabby got up from her table and came toward me to give me a hug. I was in such a rush that I overlooked her. As we walked out, Alma yelled at me, "Didn't you see who got up to say hello?" And I said, "No." Alma told me Gabby had tried to greet me and I had just kept walking, so I went back into the café to say hello. Gabby laughed because I apologized profusely. Mark was having lunch with her, and so were her parents, Gloria and Spencer. I had probably met Mark two dozen times at that point, and he still would say, "Nice to meet you."

I had met Gloria only a handful of times before. She didn't remember me, but Spencer did and he spoke to me in Spanish (his Spanish is fluent) and asked how my mother was doing. He remembered my parents from the debate. They were all very nice, and I let them get back to their lunch.

The night before the general election, we had a traditional midnight run. Fifteen or twenty of us gathered at Steve's house, and he gave us coffee and Mexican Coca-Cola that is made with real cane sugar and has more caffeine. Then we went to the different polling locations and put up signs saying, FARLEY FOR STATE REPRESENTATIVE, and signs for Gabby, and Terry Goddard, who was running for governor. We didn't put up signs for Nancy and Cheryl because they were running in a different district. Steve said it was fun because he was done by about one a.m., and he and volunteers went back to his house for dessert and more coffee. But I stayed out till four a.m., checking to see if the signs were still up, because people (I assume volunteers for the other candidates) were knocking them down. I had to put up forty-eight Gabby signs twice between midnight and four in the morning.

As usual there was an election-night party. Most of the results came in at the same time. Steve won, and we celebrated. As Alma said, our work had paid off. She and my mom had made victory cakes for Steve and Gabby in the hopes that they would win. But Gabby's election was still too close to call. Our other two candidates, Nancy and Cheryl, lost. We had put in a lot of work for them and felt disappointed.

Unlike the election in 2008, when there had been much to celebrate, 2010 was very somber. In the course of the evening the cake my mom had made for Gabby had been left on the main stage of the party and had not been taken up to her private gathering as it was supposed to have been. I didn't want to bother Gabby, but I also didn't want the cake that she had requested with her favorite flavors to be left and thrown out. So, with Kelly and Steve, I took the cake up to her suite in the hotel.

As I walked in, the mood was gray. Everyone was either quiet or crying. The results weren't looking good. Computers were open and the polling was really close. Polls showed Jesse Kelly one point ahead, then dead even with Gabby, and then Gabby was one point behind. I just wanted to drop off the cake and get out of the way. As we were getting ready to leave, Gabby came out of the bedroom portion of the suite.

She was calm—eerily calm for someone on the verge of losing her position. She came over and gave me a hug. Softly she said, "Win or lose, it's not about having power. It is about using the responsibility you are given to represent people to the best of our abilities. We will help people until the last minute I am in office. And then, after, I will continue to try to help others."

I was exhausted and saddened by the results for people like Nancy and Cheryl, but in this small moment all of my faith in the importance of public service returned. Even in this trying moment Gabby was imparting the lesson that there is more to life than just politics. Life is about helping others. This gave me faith once more in her, and in the fact that people like her who value public service are the type of people we should be electing to Congress.

That night I talked to her office manager, Joni Jones, and arranged an interview to apply for an internship in Gabby's congressional office if she were reelected.

Almost a week later we still didn't know who had won. We constantly checked the website of the secretary of state to see.

CHAPTER TWENTY-TWO
STUDENT BODY PRESIDENT

FOR YEARS I HAD BEEN PLANNING TO RUN FOR STUDENT BODY president at U of A, the university I loved. I wanted to continue working on things that I had been working on with ASA, advocating for students.

I began recruiting friends to run with me: Erik Lundstrom, who had also worked on a coordinated campaign for Gabby; Monica Ruiz and Brittany Steinke, who I knew from the Associated Students of the University of Arizona (ASUA) office; and Chandni Patel, who I hadn't known before but who had been recommended. We called ourselves Team Red. There was no particular reason why we chose red, but the color would associate us wherever we went. Erik and Chandni were running for senate, Monica was running for executive vice president, and Brittany wanted to be

Gabby was in her office when a big press release announced her very narrow victory. I was thrilled. We all were. As soon as the news came through, Gabby's staff called an impromptu party at her office. Everybody was there to celebrate: staffers, interns, Steve, Nancy, Cheryl, everyone who had worked on Gabby's campaign.

I wanted to continue working for her. She had one of the best constituent-service operations in the country. Gabby really listened to the concerns of the people in her district and had one of the highest success rates of meeting constituents' needs. She was passionate about helping others. From Gabby I learned that you don't have to have a stethoscope to help people. Public service can take many different forms, and we can all find our own ways to contribute to the betterment of society.

Gabby and her husband,
Mark Kelly, with
"Giffords for Congress" cake
on election night 2010

administrative vice president. As a slate we worked together.

I knew how to run a campaign because of my experience as Steve's campaign manager, so I took charge. The primary was coming up in early 2011, and the election was going to be held in March. I told Joni Jones, Gabby's office manager, during the interview for the internship that my time would be limited, and I asked her and Gabby to work with my schedule.

Campaigning with Monica, Chandni, and Brittany

I needed the internship for school credit, but most of all I wanted to work for and with Gabby. Halfway through the interview I was hired. Since I was one of the more qualified applicants, Joni had me doing more advanced work, like some of the staffers. I was supposed to start on January 12, when school began.

Meanwhile I turned my attention to my campaign for student body president. There was a four-hundred-dollar limit on campaign spending, and I began to plan how to raise money for handouts with my name and information about the upcoming election. Emily Fritze was the current student body president, and she had also interned for Gabby.

On December 23, I went out for dinner with Steve, Kelly, Amelia, GiGi, and my sisters, and we bumped into Gabby. She walked into the restaurant and came over to our table and sat down and talked to us for a few minutes before joining her parents. They were sitting in a back corner, so we hadn't seen them. Gabby was smiling and excited to have won the reelection. "Oh, aren't you interning in my office?" she asked me. Joni had told her, and had also said that I was planning to run for student body president, like Emily. So Gabby said, "Now there will be two Giffords interns as presidents. Let's hope we start a legacy of Giffords interns who go on to become presidents."

She also asked how my mother was and said, "Tell her to come with you to the next event."

On January 3, I got a call from Gabby's office asking me to start my internship early. They were short-staffed and needed help. So I worked in the office every day that week, answering the phone, working on constituent cases, helping the staffers with what they needed.

I also had a job working as a cashier at World Market, a

store that sells a lot of imported items. It was after the holidays and there was a break at school. I had the time, and I needed to make some money.

Dinner at a restaurant to celebrate Daniel's mother's birthday. Seated from left to right: Steve, GiGi, Amelia, Alma, Mrs. Hernandez, and Mr. Hernandez. Standing from left to right: Kelly, Consuelo, and Daniel.

On Thursday, January 6, Gabby's office got a call from her in Washington, DC, saying she wanted to do a Congress on Your Corner event. It usually takes about a week to put one together, from what I've been told, but a Safeway market in Tucson said they could do it in two days. So the staff called ten thousand homes in the area to let them know of the upcoming event. These were robo calls. Gabby recorded the message in Washington, and a program automatically dialed the phone numbers. The staff had a list of phone numbers that had zip codes that matched the zip code where the event was happening.

I offered to help out. On Friday they told me where the

event would be, the Safeway at the corner of Ina and Oracle. Afterward, I planned on depositing my financial aid check for school, paying my cell phone bill, and picking up my contact lenses. At noon or whenever the event ended, I was supposed to go to work at the World Market. If there was a crowd Gabby would rarely leave, even if she would be late to the next event.

That morning I got up at seven forty-five like I usually do. Saturday, January 8, 2011, started like an ordinary day.

Part Four

~ AFTERMATH ~

CHAPTER TWENTY-THREE
HISPANIC AND GAY

THE ROLE I PLAYED ON JANUARY 8 CHANGED MY LIFE FOREVER. Kelly said I became "globally known." I was bombarded by the media and flown to New York for live television interviews. Kelly pushed me to accept them all. I had to tell and retell the story of how I elevated Gabby, put pressure on her wound, and kept her engaged. Most of the other "early responders" gave seven or eight interviews, and some of the people who had been involved wouldn't talk about it at all.

Wherever I went, people recognized me. They came up to me and said how helpful it was in their recovery to hear my story. I've also learned to let them share their stories as well.

Kids called me an angel and asked if they could touch me. In restaurants they'd ask for my autograph. Kids liked to take pictures with me. A lot of them just wanted to come up and say hello. It was usually followed by, "My mom thinks you're brave [or nice]."

Teenagers would say, "I really admire you. You're great. It's very good what you did." They usually ask for pictures to put on Facebook or Twitter. Some of them don't think to ask but take a picture when I'm not ready. I'll be talking and in the middle of a sentence, or eating. At gas stations strangers wanted to shake my hand. In coffee shops I'd go to pay for my drink and the cashier's eyes would light up and she or he would say, "I thought you looked familiar. You're Daniel. Thank you so much." My friends acted the same as before. They didn't treat me any differently. But on the campus of U of A, students stopped to hug me.

It got to be too much. Especially when I was running late to everything. I would spend ten minutes talking to someone instead of getting into my car and driving away as I should have. I tried to be accommodating. I would get stopped for radio or television interviews. But I didn't want to be the focus of attention. I don't want to be in the limelight.

People came by to take pictures of my house. My parents weren't very happy now that they were the subject of scrutiny. Reporters would stop my mother more than they'd stop the other members of my family. She and I did one TV interview together in Spanish on the Spanish network, Univision. Right away my mom and I heard from family members in Mexico. They started calling to see what was going on. Some thought they deserved attention and that this was an opportunity to get money and become famous. They assumed that because I was doing so much media that I was making a lot of money, which I wasn't.

Daniel at a Victory Fund event with Congresswoman Sheila Jackson Lee (left, front) and New York City Council speaker Christine Quinn (right, front).

In the first few days after the shooting, I received hundreds of e-mails. Not all the messages were positive. There were hurtful remarks. Some people wrote nasty things.

"You're too fat. Get off my TV."

"You're too brown. Go back to your country."

"You're going to hell." Apparently because I'm gay.

The Dallas Voice, a media source for LGBT readers in Texas, had posted an interview with me the morning after the shooting and had identified me as a "gay intern." An LGBT website quoted the Dallas article and further identified me as "a gay Latino."

Some comments were supportive, though. "The fact that Mr. Hernandez is a homosexual and a Hispanic needs to be pointed out." And, "LGBT Americans do heroic things just like straight Americans."

However, one woman from Washington, DC, wrote, "It would be a mistake for anyone to draw the conclusion that because a person described as 'gay' does laudable things, that homosexuality is, therefore, not abnormal. It is abnormal." She added that homosexuality and transgenderism "are preventable and treatable," and provided me with links to websites with descriptors such as "gay to straight" and "people can change."

The Tucson LGBT commission was receiving these kinds of e-mails too, and the co-chair sent a message to all of the commissioners advising us to contact the police with anything serious. "This is a crazy world," she wrote, "and unfortunately many commissioners are getting negative e-mails from individuals referencing Daniel and his sexual orientation. Please do not respond to any of these e-mails. It may be wise to not read them."

Kelly got upset and said, "I just stopped reading the blogs. It's hard being gay and a Hispanic in Arizona."

But hurtful remarks don't stay with me. I don't pay attention. I have a very thick skin. I've always been this way. I don't get defensive about myself. I get defensive about other people I care about, like family, the congresswoman, or other candidates that I've worked with or for. If they're getting attacked, that's when I get upset. I'm sensitive about other people; I'm not so sensitive about myself.

I received positive messages too, and people wrote nice things like, "Thank you," "Bless you!" and "Love you."

One of my classmates at the university had seen my interview on CNN the day after the shooting and wrote, "I'm proud to say that I took Japanese 102 with this person."

Julia Ashley, a Reiki Master in Ohio, wrote, "I wanted to share with you a medical study that suggests you did more for Gabby than you suspect. You may have lessened her pain as well." Julia quoted a paper by a French cardiologist and said that I should consider taking up alternative healing as well as poli-sci. "I believe healing will call you again," she wrote. "You can do both, just don't rule out alternative medicine, you are a natural."

The amount of correspondence I was receiving was overwhelming. I have a file of hundreds of e-mails. After a while I didn't check my e-mails for six months. Then I basically started a new e-mail account. I didn't like any of the attention, whether it was positive or negative.

The only time I care is when it's a threat of some kind, like when I was asked to speak somewhere and someone wrote, "If you ever come back to my town again, I'm going to make sure you regret it." I report threats of violence to the proper authorities. It depends on where the person's coming from. It's important to let people know they can't make threats idly and get away with it. I haven't gotten any death threats yet.

But there were also letters from kids all over the map who faced identity crises. They'd write, "I never thought I would be able to get an education, but because of what you said . . ." Or, "I never thought someone who was Latino could . . . ," and they'd mention one of the things I had done.

I am also given credit for a lot of things I've never done, like going up in a space shuttle with Mark. I'm apparently a very good singer. I have a very, very nice car. I live in a very, very nice home outside of Tucson in either New York or DC, and I have lots of money. I don't sleep. (That one, for the most part, is true.)

I get letters from older women who are grandmothers who say, "Oh, you would be perfect for my . . . ," and they insert the name of a grandchild. They give me the names of young men as well as women. I've had people who've offered to set me up with other people. It's not something I'm interested in; I don't even have time for myself.

People send gifts, mostly cards and letters expressing condolences or congratulations. I've been given a few interesting items, none of which I've kept. I either return them or give them to Gabby's office. The office handles them. I don't want to be seen as taking advantage of what happened by accepting free drinks, free dinners, or free desserts.

In those first days and weeks after the shooting, I had no updates on Gabby's condition except what her office staff gave for public releases. At the memorial ceremony at the University of Arizona on January 12, President Obama had told us that Gabby had opened her eyes for the first time after he'd stopped by to visit her in the hospital. She had miraculously survived the gunshot wound and brain surgery. I knew Gabby was going to make it, but no one knew what lay ahead for her during her recovery. Later I learned that after the surgery she was hooked up to a tracheotomy tube. But by January 19 she came out of a medically induced coma and was taken off the ventilator.

At each announcement of her progress, the media besieged me for my reactions. When reporters asked me what I thought about her recovery and political future, I said, "The thing I care most about is her as a person."

I still wore the silver Virgin Mary icon that her mother had given me. And we all started wearing turquoise-colored rubber bracelets with the words, "Peace. Love. Gabby." Turquoise is her favorite color. The bracelets went on sale in February 2011 for one dollar apiece. The proceeds go to the Gabe Zimmerman Memorial Scholarship of Arizona State University School of Social Work for the master's program. I bought twenty-five. Some I gave away. I keep breaking them, and once a bracelet breaks, I just pull out a new one and wear it. I wore a bracelet all through the spring and summer, and when I was out campaigning door-to-door, a tan line formed on my wrist.

I tried to carry on with my life, but the tragedy stayed with me. The memories will be something I'll have to live with for a long time.

Sometimes people have agendas. I recall an incident where a reporter tried to shadow me in everything that I did. I rebuffed his requests, thinking I didn't want my already open life to be more public and for me to lose any sense of privacy I had left. It seemed as though this reporter wanted to paint me as an extremist Latino activist, which is, of course, not the case. He would interview people with leading questions, and my impression was that when he didn't get what he wanted, he changed it to, "Daniel Hernandez is a radical LGBT activist," which, once again, is not the case. One of the reasons I've been successful in politics is because of my carefully thought-out way of expressing myself. While I understand the need for extremism, I am and have always been a moderate.

The reporter was frustrated that he couldn't sensationalize me further, and tried a new angle. "Daniel Hernandez is depressed." He did an interview with my family and titled the piece, GIFFORDS' INTERN STRUGGLES TO COPE WITH ARIZONA TRAGEDY. It appeared on the front page of the paper and upset me. The reporter asked leading questions and guided my parents and sisters into saying what he wanted for the story.

He said to my sister Consuelo, "Daniel must have changed emotionally because of the shooting."

And he quoted her as saying, "I worry about him all the time. Psychologically, I know he has changed. Things like that you will never forget."

The reporter wrote, "The typically open and outgoing Hernandez has withdrawn emotionally from those closest to him, say his family and friends. His friends and family worry that . . . Hernandez is hiding from the emotions he has kept bottled up since a gunman shot 19 people, killing six, outside a Safeway on Jan. 8."

He also interviewed my friends David and Elma. David said that I did not talk to him about the shootings. Elma said about me, "He's coping well, but I do worry about him a lot."

I felt violated. I was mad that I had let somebody in to talk to my parents, sisters, and friends. Kelly had pushed me into doing it. We were accepting all of the interviews, but this was the one we regretted. I knew that there would be a time when the press would turn on me. However, I had hoped that the change would be because of something I had done, not because of something that they wished I had done.

I saw a grief counselor only briefly. The day after the shooting, Gabby's office manager wrote to all of us and said there would be a grief counselor on-site for anyone who would like extra help getting through this. She also told us about stress debriefings and special sessions for our staff that were being offered that first week in Tucson.

I met this counselor on multiple occasions, but we agreed that I didn't need to go continuously. There was nothing that she could tell me to do that I wasn't already doing. Everyone copes differently, and I had coped well. Having to talk about it as often as I had and in front of others had allowed me to process and deal with the tragic events.

The other survivors and I grew close. The bonds are very strong. I don't have nightmares. I don't have the traumatic flashbacks that some of the others have—but when I do talk about it, I remember the gunshots.

Daniel and his parents (seated) at a United States Hispanic Media Coalition event at which Daniel was honored. Standing left to right: Zoë Saldana, Daniel, Vikki Carr, Lupita Quinones, and Danny Trejo

Chapter Twenty-four
My Mother's List

Starting in late January, I received many invitations from groups all over the country to accept awards and give speeches. At first I was surprised. I wasn't expecting any of it. I found that I enjoyed motivational speaking more than interviews; it helped me feel like I was giving back by sharing my story.

Kelly got the requests and asked her friend and colleague Carole Pearsall, a Democratic activist, to help schedule me. I looked at every invitation individually and checked the calendar. If I had appointments on campus for my campaign for student body president of U of A, then I would stay and not travel.

I was dividing my time between the campaign and interning at Gabby's office. The internship fulfilled my credits for school. I'd spend about six hours twice a week doing constituent casework, whatever needed to be done—phone calls, letter writing, preparing papers. Gabby's staff had opened the office two days after the shooting and wanted to continue her work, being there for the constituents. Hundreds of new cases came in, including issues on student loans.

On January 21, Gabby left University Medical Center in Tucson and was flown to Houston to begin rehabilitation near her husband, Mark. He was preparing to command the final mission of the space shuttle *Endeavour*. I was getting ready to go to Washington, DC, for the president's State of the Union address.

My next trip to Washington came soon after. LULAC (the League of United Latin American Citizens) invited me to their annual gala in Washington, DC. I brought my mom, since she had never been to Washington before.

Daniel at the gala for the League of United Latin American Citizens

At the LULAC event I was awarded the Presidential Citation, a medal on a ribbon. It was especially meaningful to me because my mom was there. When we got home, she put the medal in a glass-fronted cabinet near the TV in the living room. From then on she started collecting my awards. (My mom's list is at the back of the book.)

Another honor that meant a lot to me was the Theodore Roosevelt Award for Outstanding Public Service. This was given to me by the OPM (the United States Office of Personnel Management) in Washington, DC. At the event I spoke about America's youth. I talked about diversity issues and how we should take care of them now so that when young people grow up, they can assume leadership roles whether they're African American or Asian, gay or straight.

OPM Director John Berry presented me with a little bust of Teddy Roosevelt cast in metal. For me this was truly an honor.

Out magazine chose me as one of the "men and women who made 2011 a year to remember." Each of us was featured on a page in the magazine.

I was flown to Los Angeles for the photo session. It wasn't the first time I'd been photographed for a magazine. I had been interviewed for *GQ* right after the shooting, and the article had been published with a picture of me that made me look especially handsome and well dressed. This struck me as funny, because I'm not someone who cares a lot about my appearance.

For the issue of *Out* magazine, all the photographs were

based on famous portraits from the twentieth century. They took a picture of me duplicating the pose of Richard Nixon that appeared on the cover of *Esquire* magazine in May 1968, when he was running for president. Like Nixon, I'm in profile with my eyes closed, and the hands of stylists are in view as they spray my hair, powder my face, and apply lipstick.

In the caption they wrote that I was active in LGBT and education issues, and had been raising awareness and funds for various causes. An awards ceremony sponsored by Buick was going to be held in New York. I was invited to attend, but I had another commitment. I had promised to do something for Judge Rolls's family. He was one of the people killed on January 8, and his son's wife had invited me to speak at an open house at the school where she teaches. I was using the attention I was getting to reach out to young people and try to make a difference.

Chapter Twenty-five
TEAM RED

Because of what happened on January 8, and my exposure in the media, I had name recognition and a lot of good will. This helped me in my campaign to become ASUA president. My friends Erik, Chandni, Monica, and Brittany worked with me on Team Red. My sisters, Alma and Consuelo, helped too. Consuelo was a student at U of A studying premed. We all wore red T-shirts with the words "Vote Team Red: Hernandez for President" printed in black. In addition to running Steve's campaign for the state representative, I had also run Emily Fritze's campaign for student president, and she had been elected. As outgoing president she was in charge of running the election and had to be fair, so she couldn't come out for me or anybody else. But as a friend she was supportive, and occasionally she gave me advice.

Our biggest job was to recruit volunteers. We had to collect enough signatures from students at the university to qualify me to get on the ballot: four hundred names by February. I cut back on my travel so that I could work with my team. We couldn't do any campaigning until after the primary.

Three people were running for the primary. The top two would move on to the general election. My strongest opponent was a young man who was Emily's chief of staff. He belonged to a fraternity and had the Greek life members behind him as a voting bloc. Pledges automatically worked for him, whereas we had to call up volunteers. We knocked on doors, sent e-mails and text messages, and made phone calls.

I made it to the primary, and then the real campaigning began. Team Red had to do it all over again: knock on doors, send e-mails, make phone calls, and hand out literature. I would go to events on campus like club meetings (there are about five hundred clubs), introduce myself, and talk about my work on student advocacy and trying to prevent budget cuts. Tuition was going to go up, and it was important to work with the state legislature and get things done.

I took part in a debate and discussed how we would help lower university costs. In a way it was "frat boys against the students." But I went to Greek houses and sometimes convinced the kids there to vote for me. My opponent accused me of being a blatant opportunist, anti-Greek, and a slew of other things, none of which was true. He said I had a big head and a record of not caring about the students. I let him keep doing what he was doing and wouldn't sink to his level.

Meanwhile, because of January 8, I kept receiving invitations to attend events and awards ceremonies, but I accepted few of them. My main focus was the campaign and interning in Gabby's office.

The student body election was held from March 7 to 9, and students voted online. We found out that my opponent had people pressuring voters by standing over their laptops and telling them how to vote. On election night we gathered in the student union and waited for the results. A picture in the *Arizona Republic* shows me hugging two of my hardworking teammates, Monica and Brittany. I asked my parents not to come that evening, but Alma and Consuelo brought them anyway. Kelly and Steve were also there. Many people thought I would automatically win.

Daniel with Team Red on ASUA election night

Finally Emily stood up to announce the results. My opponent and I were both disqualified. Neither of us had won. We were charged with breaking the election codes and exceeding the maximum of ten election violations.

For a moment I was stunned, but I tried to remain stoic. Kelly later said that for the first time she saw me flustered. She felt sick for me.

The next day we heard the charges. I was accused of infractions such as giving out 150 "Vote Team Red" T-shirts to students on the Mall, and thus being responsible when a student was seen wearing the shirt in the ASUA office, which is nonpartisan and off-limits for campaigning. I should have informed this person of the rules, according to the charges. Another complaint against me was that my team and I had purposely left flyers on the tables and in the study rooms in the Integrated Learning Center at the university Main Library, and that we had placed posters in "close proximity" to university computer labs, an area off-limits because they represent polling stations. It took forty-eight hours to investigate. My opponent used questionable campaign tactics. Emily knew it and was very annoyed. I had run an honest campaign. I did not willingly break the rules. I had relied on volunteers who were told the regulations but had misplaced posters. I was determined to fight it out.

We both had to appear before the student supreme court to have the charges lifted. The hearing on March 29 was widely attended. I represented myself and argued my case. My opponent hired a professional attorney.

After a careful review of the evidence, the elections commissioner wrote, "I have deemed Mr. Hernandez's actions to not be severely detrimental to the election process." However, the commissioner judged that my opponent's actions were "severely detrimental to the election process." As a result, he stated, the race had been compromised, and "the only fair outcome of this proceeding is a special election."

So a special election was set for a few weeks later. My opponent was allowed to run, since he had received the most votes in the first general election. Three new candidates joined us on the ballot.

I restarted everything from scratch, visiting the clubs all over again, explaining what had happened, and telling students about the special election. But my opponent again used questionable tactics. Yet, according to the way the election code was written, his penalties would not have added up to grounds for disqualifying him. There wasn't much we could do. On April 22 he won the election and was announced as the ASUA president.

I was angry and disappointed at the way it had turned out. But it wasn't worth challenging him.

Kelly and Steve said to me, "This is not your platform anymore. Your life has changed."

I had a lot more important things that I could do on a state and national level.

Chapter Twenty-six
Talking to Kids

Right after the special election for ASUA student body president, I carried on with school appearances. I felt strongly about talking to young people. I accepted hundreds of invitations to give keynote addresses, speeches, and informal talks in Arizona, as well as in other parts of the country. I received no money for 95 percent of these appearances. My travel expenses were usually paid for by my hosts or nonprofit organizations, but if I drove to a distant part of Arizona, like Douglas, I often paid for gas myself.

Sometimes I'm given specific themes or topics, or I'm asked to motivate kids for an upcoming exam or challenge. Whatever they ask me to talk about, I do. If I am talking to older students, I encourage them to register to vote. It varies. I don't prepare; I just talk.

Often I speak about diversity, what it means to live in the Southwest. Tucson is a diverse city with people coming in from all over the world. We have refugees from Korea, Africa, Cambodia, Laos, and Sudan. We see how people from many cultures can work together.

I've spoken to different groups, usually ages fourteen to twenty, about education, taking advantage of every opportunity, making the best use of their time, and being willing to put in hard work. I talk about getting involved in student government or politics or the church. People come up afterward and ask me questions about things I've done, if I know how they can get involved with causes that interest them. Sometimes they ask for advice about things they're working on.

In April, I spoke at a career fair at the Tucson High Magnet School and talked about the value of higher education, and the importance of public service, giving back to the community. I returned to the school as a keynote speaker when they held a first responders youth career day. First responders handle emergency medical situations. About five hundred high school students and graduates attended this event, which gave them a chance to get information about training programs and certification.

At Douglas High School, in Douglas, Arizona, near the border of Mexico, I talked to students and told them that they could make a difference. "The younger you are, you actually have more power, because you'll be around longer," I said. I spoke about my interest in politics and how I had worked for Gabby, and before that for Hillary Clinton's 2008 presidential campaign. I said that I thought women had the ability to listen and compromise.

"Government is all about compromise; no one ever gets exactly what they want. But I feel men are less willing to find a solution because they are more concerned about being right than they are willing to get things done."

Kids may have been surprised by my attitude. But Gabby had always believed that if more women served in government, compromise on issues would come more easily.

She had often visited stretches of the U.S.-Mexican border in her district, and was concerned about fixing the immigration system. "We have two border problems," she said, "security and reform of our broken immigration laws. . . . We can and we must address both of these problems."

Gabby and I had talked about these issues privately, but I never spoke about immigration to students. My messages focused on education and public service.

My family often went back and forth to Nogales, Sonora. It was usually smooth and easy. But I know others who had had issues. People who are American citizens who don't speak English well or at all are discriminated against. These are mostly the older ones, even though they were born here. Younger people generally learn English. Friends of my mother's and her family members weren't citizens, so border patrol agents asked them questions pertaining to coming into the country.

I had only one bad experience crossing the border. When I was about ten or eleven, we took a trip to Nogales, Mexico, for the wedding of one of my mother's friend's sons. The entire trip was completely uncomfortable. Mexican police threatened to put drugs into our car unless we paid them off, and my father had to do it. I was annoyed with how corrupt the police were. I've always had problems with corruption at all levels, whether it's local, federal, state—it doesn't matter. Corruption is always the same.

When I speak to kids, they usually want to hear about January 8 and what happened. "Ten minutes into the event starting, someone came in with a gun and started firing," I say. When I tell them about what I did for Gabby, I say, "I had a little bit of training but not much."

I meet a lot of Latino kids. Most of them talk about how they don't have a role model to look up to. I try to respond but rarely have time to interact as I want to.

Kids always ask the same questions:

"Who's your favorite person who you've met so far?"

"What was it like to meet the president?"

"What was it like to sit *next* to the president?"

And I always give the same answer. "It was a very surreal thing."

Then they ask about the shooting. "Was it scary?" "Did

you see the gunman?" "Why didn't you run away?"

And I say, "I had training, and I wanted to help the people who had been injured."

Then I often get, "Why aren't you married? Do you have any children?"

I never envisioned myself having kids. I think I would be a horrible parent. My expectations would be too high. And I'd never be home.

Most of the kids in school audiences don't know how old I am. I usually tell them my age, and then they back off, because I'm a lot younger than they think I am.

Sometimes they ask about my personal life, but I'm very cautious about what I share. I'm always careful in terms of knowing my audience, like when I was in Douglas. It has a large Latino population, and many registered Democrats live there. That was a very different audience from the one in Tombstone, Arizona. Tombstone has 15 percent registered Democrats, and the rest are Republicans, with a lot of military families.

I don't receive put-downs, but I do get what I call obnoxious questions. Oftentimes a teenager who thinks he knows more than I do will try to throw me off by asking an inappropriate or completely irrelevant question. But I'm good on my feet, and I usually go back to whatever I'm talking about, so no matter what they bring up, I make sure I stay on message.

This happened in Douglas. The high school audience was

not very participatory. The kids needed a little coaxing to come out of their shells. So I asked them, "What are the biggest issues that you guys are facing down here in Douglas?"

One young man stood up. He seemed upset and started talking about fascists and racists, trying to throw me off, when we were trying to have a productive conversation. So I was able to tie in what he said, phrasing it in a less inflammatory way than he had. Later the principal told me that the boy was a problematic student and often did things like that.

Kids don't talk personally in front of a big group, but afterward they'll talk privately to me about their problems. In middle school they complain about their teachers, and in high school they ask for programs that have been cut.

At Camp Pride in Nashville, Tennessee, I received an honorary Voice and Action National Leadership Award. This recognition meant a lot to me because it was about social justice advocacy and diversity education. The program brought together sixty LGBT young people from around the country for five days of student leadership development. Shane L. Windmeyer, the founder and executive director of Campus Pride, has published books about gay campus issues. He said that my service to the Tucson LGBT community and my work with Gabby had inspired young students across the country, and he praised me for "doing the right, just thing and being visible.

"In a time where we have national headlines about LGBT

youth suicide," said Shane, "it is even more important to shine a light on young adult leaders like Daniel who give hope and inspire." I felt good about that.

In May, I was particularly honored to speak at graduation ceremonies at Sunnyside High School, the school I had attended, and at Desert View High School and S.T.A.R. Academic Center, also part of the Sunnyside school district. It was a great chance to encourage kids in a neighborhood that was still mainly Latino to go on to college and get higher education. "We all have the power to make things happen; we all have the opportunity to change things," I said. "It's just what we choose to do with those opportunities."

People started talking to me about running for the Sunnyside District School Board because of advocacy work I had done in education. Sunnyside was my district, so it made sense. In June, I decided to do it.

Chapter Twenty-seven
School Board

I MADE UP MY MIND TO RUN FOR SCHOOL BOARD AT THE LAST MIN-
ute, two days before signatures had to be collected to get my
name on the ballot. I have a strange way of operating. I'm a big
procrastinator. My best work gets done under pressure. It may
not be the best way for everyone, but it works for me.

I had lived in the Sunnyside school district my entire life,
so I knew the challenges facing the schools. The district is
80 percent Latino. The demographics have always been the
same. I knew how important it was to talk about some of the
needs of students and families that don't always get addressed.
Especially because I'm on the younger side, I would get a
chance to see and experience things that people who have been
on the board for twenty years don't get a chance to see. So
when I was recruited to run for school board, I thought it was

a good opportunity to lend my voice to those who didn't oftentimes get heard. I'd already worked on education issues. Now
I switched from higher education to K through 12.

The district is plagued with problems. Only 60 percent of
the students graduate. The rest still live in the neighborhood.
They're just not getting educated, and that is the problem.
They can't pass their classes, or they choose not to. They just
stop going to school and get involved in drugs, violence, steal-
ing, and general crime. I wanted to work on improving our
continuance program so people who left school could return.
As long as they're under the age of twenty-one, they're eligible to receive a public education. The goal was finding people
who had dropped out when they were sixteen or seventeen
and, now that they were eighteen or nineteen, getting them to
come back so they could finish their education. It was like this
when I was a student. I wanted to get involved and fix things. I
wanted things to be better for my sisters and their future kids.

That summer I began preparing for the school board race. I
was taking two classes for each part of the summer session at U
of A. I gave up my position as LGBT commissioner because I
didn't want to have too many things on my plate, and I needed
to focus on getting elected, then making sure I had the time to
serve.

In May, I had stopped interning at Gabby's office. But I
stayed in touch and would see people from her staff at different events. I learned through press releases that Gabby was

slowly improving at the rehabilitation hospital in Houston. Newspapers reported that doctors called her progress "quite remarkable" and "almost miraculous." She was speaking a little and able to say a few words and phrases. In May, I talked to her over the phone for the first time since the tragedy. Our conversation lasted less than a minute, but I heard her voice and she heard mine.

In late April, she had been allowed to fly to Florida for the scheduled launch of the space shuttle *Endeavour*, commanded by her husband, Mark. But the mission was scrubbed because of an electrical problem. And when Gabby and Mark returned to Houston, they went out to dinner at a restaurant for Mother's Day. The outing was a big news story on TV. Anytime something happened to Gabby, the media contacted me to get my reactions. By June, I had conducted more than five hundred media interviews in English and Spanish with local, state, national, and international outlets.

Reporters and interviewers also asked my opinion about justice for the accused shooter, Jared Loughner.

On March 9, Loughner had appeared in federal court in Tucson. He had been indicted on charges of murder and attempted murder, for a total of forty-nine counts against him. I was "victim number thirty-three," one of the people he had put at risk while we'd been exercising our fundamental right to assemble freely, openly, and peacefully with our member of Congress. I didn't attend that hearing, but I do go to some of the hearings with others who were involved in the January 8 shooting. We had become a tight-knit group and kept track of what everyone was doing, with phone calls and e-mails. Until all of us are gone, the bonds that tie us will remain very strong. I'm the youngest of the group by far. The only person close to my age is an intern who ran away that morning.

On May 25, a judge declared Loughner mentally unfit to stand trial. He was being held for mental evaluation at a hospital for federal prisoners in Missouri. On September 28, it was decided to keep him on forced medications for three months to see if there would be an emotional change by the end of 2011.

When asked for my comment, I said, "I am not a lawyer. I am not a judge. It's not my place to say how he should be punished."

I only expressed hope that we could move to act on the good we saw coming from this tragedy.

Chapter Twenty-eight
VOTE DANIEL HERNANDEZ

When I ran for the Sunnyside school board, my whole family was excited. I appointed my sister Alma as my campaign manager. She says she was scared at the beginning. But I wanted her to get experience and to give her a chance to grow as a staffer. I thought she would benefit as we headed for the 2012 election season. Alma was eighteen and interested in politics. She still had a lot of learning to do and wasn't where she needed to be to do the job at the level I wanted. I really ran the campaign.

We had no campaign headquarters. We just worked wherever was convenient at the time: out of my home, her place (an apartment she shared with roommates), sometimes a coffee shop, in my car—a little bit of everything.

She and I went door-to-door in the Sunnyside district. We

had volunteers, too. Alma is good at recruiting volunteers, which is important in a small local race. She said, "I was convincing students that they needed to get involved. The challenge is getting people motivated."

And people came to us and told us they were interested in helping. A group of my former teachers went door-to-door for me and made several hundred phone calls on my behalf. I did most of my own walking, knocking on doors and talking to people who lived in the district. Alma's job included returning e-mails to people who donated money for the campaign (we had a limit of $430 per individual), and calling voters to see if they would support me.

There are about seventy-nine thousand people in the Sunnyside district, including my parents. We had information that helped us decide which houses to go to. There are about thirty-thousand registered voters, and we knew who had been voting in local elections. People who vote in local elections are pretty plugged in as to what is going on, so we contacted the ones who had voted in the previous election. We didn't waste time. We were very precise regarding who we were talking to and which points we made with certain people.

I prepared a script for the campaign. I didn't need to write it for myself but for others. I stated the points of what I hoped to accomplish. Bullying was not as high a priority as some of the other goals, like full-day kindergarten, an issue important to a vast majority of the voters. Steve took a picture of me (in a blue shirt and tie) and printed it on a campaign mailer that he designed. I wanted the flyer to be bilingual. One side was written in English, and the other was in Spanish.

Mailer for Daniel's school board campaign

The bullet points read:

- Protect all-day kindergarten to serve our kids
- Partner with the local business community
- Produce college- and workforce-ready high school seniors

We sent the flyer to six thousand homes in the district. It said, "Vote Daniel Hernandez, Mail by November 1." For this election people had to send in their ballots.

The board has five members. There were two vacancies. One was appointed and one was to be elected.

I thought, *If I'm not there to fight for kids and teachers, then who else will?* A former police officer ran against me, and a disgruntled employee of the district also entered the race.

My opponents started spreading rumors about me and attacking my character. "What qualifies him?" they said. They thought I didn't know anything about education. They said I didn't care enough about kids and was going to use this position as a stepping-stone in my political career. They made sly insults and said I wasn't "manly enough" to be on the school district board.

But people were disgusted and stood up for me.

"How dare you attack him?" they said. "He is of the highest moral caliber."

My actions spoke for themselves. Even during my experience running for student body president at U of A, people tended to defend me when I was attacked. I'm like Teflon. I have nonstick coating, and the attacks slide off me.

During the race I made no mention of my role in the January 8 shooting. On my website I said only that I had worked on Congresswoman Giffords's 2008 congressional campaign. But it was a problem. High name recognition came with some high negatives. When I was campaigning, people recognized me and would say, "I know you from the January 8 rampage, but how does that qualify you to be a school board member?"

I talked about how I had been involved in education advocacy for some time. My main concern at first had been higher education, but my attention had turned to dwindling funds for kindergarten through high school. Arizona had slashed spending per student by 24 percent since 2008. If elected as a school board member in the Sunnyside Unified School District, my top priority would be protecting all-day kindergarten.

Throughout the summer I worked hard on the campaign, walking door-to-door in the heat.

I took time out to accept invitations that came as a result of the role I had played on January 8. Some of the events were really fun, like throwing the first pitch at the San Diego Padres' baseball game. My parents and sisters went with me, and we sat in the team owner's box. Throwing a baseball in front of a large crowd is something I'm not very good at, but at least I didn't bounce the ball. Bill Badger, who had tackled the gunman on January 8, and Pat Maisch, who had grabbed the gunman's ammunition, were also honored guests at the game.

On the same day as the baseball game I was invited to be a

grand marshal in the Pride Parade in San Diego. I was told I could bring family, so they drove up. In the parade I rode in a convertible. Alma sat with me, and she took a lot of pictures. We had a chance to meet the actress Meredith Baxter, who served as a grand marshal too.

But in the fall I cut back on travel. I needed to focus on school and the campaign. I was taking six classes at U of A, including math, a requirement. It had been six years since I had taken a math class, so it was tough for me. I got a low score and had to retake the final exam.

The campaign grew more intense in the last few days. Alma said, "When you're in a campaign, you work till the very last minute. That last two or three days matter the most." We both got frustrated with each other and got into a fight. It probably was about her not doing her job as well as I wanted her to. I had high expectations, and she didn't always know how I wanted things to be done. The way Alma remembers it, I most likely asked her to do something she didn't want to do.

Alma said, "I quit."

I said, "If you leave, you can't come back."

"I don't care," she said, and started crying.

She called our mom, who called me, and we fixed the problem. Alma asked me to rehire her. I told her she needed to grow up, but I took her back.

On Election Day, Tuesday, November 8, 2011, our database showed that there were ballots that hadn't been turned in yet.

Alma and my parents called people in the district, reminding them to turn in their ballots, or offering to pick ballots up for those who couldn't deliver them. It was mainly the elderly who kept their ballots till the last minute. We were all working together, so my mom didn't even have time to bake a cake.

That evening I went to have pizza with Kelly, Steve, GiGi, Amelia, and my roommates, Kim and Ryan. I still didn't know if I had won the election, but I had a hunch that I might win, because I had done more campaigning than my opponents.

After dinner we went to the gathering of the Democratic Party at the Lodge on the Desert. My sisters and parents were already there. Alma had been busy decorating the room with balloons. At around seven p.m. the election results were shown on a big screen. And at the very end my name appeared. I had won by 63 percent of the vote. Alma was particularly proud and happy because she had been my campaign manager. "It was fun," she said.

I took multiple oaths of office. The first was during a special board meeting at seven a.m. on December 8, before the board went into executive session. Next, at a ceremonial event on Tuesday evening, December 13, I was sworn into office by the governing board clerk Magdalena Barajas at district headquarters. I raised my hand and swore to "support the Constitution of the United States and the Constitution and laws of the State of Arizona," and "to faithfully discharge the duties of the office." My parents and sisters were there, and

Steve, and some of my teachers from Liberty Elementary School. And right after the ceremony I went into a meeting.

I was now an elected representative on a nonpartisan board and was very mindful of my position. My students have needs that are very different from most other kids'. Many have a low socioeconomic status. I wanted to make sure they got the support they needed, and I intended to provide the best environment for their family members to find jobs.

I wondered if Gabby knew about my win. On November 15, I saw her on TV as she was interviewed by Diane Sawyer. It was so good to see her and hear her speak. This was the first time I had seen her since the shooting. There were no changes in her personality. She still had the same big smile.

During the interview, pictures were shown of the day of the massacre, including one of me walking alongside Gabby on the stretcher, holding her hand, as she was hurried to the ambulance. Diane Sawyer announced the publication of a memoir that Gabby and Mark had written, *Gabby: A Story of Courage and Hope*, dedicated to the memory of the six who had died that day.

In December, at a state fund-raiser for the Democratic Party in Phoenix, I saw Gabby's friend Representative Debbie Wasserman Schultz. She came over to me, and we had one-on-one time. Representative Wasserman Schultz said that she had had lunch with Gabby and had told her about the election of Greg Stanton as mayor of Phoenix, and my election. And they were both very pleased. So was I.

Chapter Twenty-nine
on the job

From December 2011 into the New Year, my life was busier than ever. I was always doing multiple things, attending classes and school board meetings. Each day I had to look at my iPad to see what I was supposed to do. Carole Pearsall, Kelly's scheduler, made up the plan of engagements and interviews for me and posted it electronically. I was constantly eating on the go, drinking on the go. I couldn't remember the last time I had just sat down and eaten without either my cell phone or my iPad, or some kind of work needing to be done.

In the month of January it was my priority to officially visit every single school site in my district, and observe. Sometimes I would just drop in on my own. I would go to Liberty Elementary, Apollo Middle School, and Sunnyside High School, where I had been a student, and sometimes I would stop by my old first-grade classroom and talk to Mrs. Martinez, who had been my teacher.

We are still figuring out the most effective way to teach English to children whose first language is Spanish. The state has mandated that there be segregated blocks of English-language learning, which separates these children from the rest of the school population.

Mrs. Martinez thinks that it's problematic to segregate the kids for three or four hours in compliance with the state law. "Kids learn from kids," she says. Recently the White House chose Sunnyside as a site for talking about education in the Latino community.

The Sunnyside district school board meets twice a month, on the second and fourth Tuesdays at six thirty p.m. We are in charge of curriculum and budgets, everything pertaining to providing services for eighteen thousand students and fifteen hundred employees. There are often emergency meetings and special meetings because of issues that have come up over the last year, like bullying.

We've had a surge of violence in one of our middle schools that is mostly Latino. People in the school came to tell us that they wouldn't be surprised if there was a death at that school, unless we addressed the amount of violence. So we're trying to find ways to address the issue without overstepping our role.

There are different kinds of bullying for many different reasons. It's all over the map—because someone is smart or gay, or "very gay," or sexy, or too fat, or too short, or too tall. The real issue is that kids who bully are not secure about themselves. So instead of addressing the problem, they lash out at others.

Another problem we have is children who have started cutting themselves as a way to cope with painful situations in their lives. We have students who have developed bulimia. We have students who are doing multiple things that are just not appropriate. Things are getting worse in middle school. It's time to set up the right tools for students to express what they feel is right or wrong. We're trying to have meetings with parents and students. My emphasis is trying to get awareness of the bullying problem. It's one of my goals. There are many things I'm trying to accomplish at the same time. We're still working on setting things up.

Part of my job as a board member is to read masses of material before the twice-monthly meetings. Sometimes the reports are six hundred pages long. And I try to get along with the four other board members, two men and two women, all older than I am. At age twenty-two I'm the youngest by far. There are many different personalities on the board, and I try to make sure that I listen to all points of view before making decisions. My objective is to build consensus.

Meanwhile, I have assigned reading for my classes at U of A to finish my senior year. And more invitations for speeches and events that Kelly accepted on my behalf. People in Tucson have started wearing white rubber bracelets impressed with the inscription, REMEMBER 1.8.11. We wore these in addition to the turquoise bracelets.

It was almost the one-year anniversary of the tragedy.

Chapter Thirty
One-Year Anniversary

SUNDAY, JANUARY 8, 2012, DID *NOT* START LIKE AN ORDINARY DAY. That morning at 10:10 a.m., the exact moment gunfire had sounded and Gabby had been shot a year before, bells tolled all around Tucson.

I learned that at the Safeway market where the shooting had taken place, people gathered with hand bells and rang them in remembrance. A small memorial had been set up at the spot where the victims had fallen. A plaque mounted on a rock base read, "Honoring the victims of the event of January 8, 2011. The Tucson Tragedy . . . we shall never forget." Once again people had left tributes: flowers, candles, little American flags, balloons printed with the words "Thinking of you," and last year's newspapers with the horrific headlines.

That afternoon I joined a gathering at St. Augustine

Cathedral for an interfaith service. One by one the names of the victims were called. In memory of Judge Rolls, I placed a rose in a vase near the altar. Memorial services were planned all over Tucson.

At three p.m. my sisters, Kelly, and I drove over to U of A and headed for Centennial Hall to attend a program titled "Reflections." On the way we were stopped by TV reporters. Satellite trucks from NBC, News 4, Univision, and ABC were lined up on the grassy mall just as they had been on the day when the president spoke at the memorial ceremony after the shooting. The CNN reporter ran up to me with a mike as I kept walking.

"How have you changed this past year?" he asked.

"Not now," I said.

"We've got to go live at the top of the hour," he said.

"I'll see you later," I called over my shoulder. "Sorry about that."

"At 6:05 we can interview you," shouted the reporter. "You can go and come back."

It was an eerie reminder of what had happened a year before, when I had been besieged by the media.

In Centennial Hall, I quietly talked with Mr. Green, the father of Christina-Taylor Green. Volunteers handed out more white bracelets that said, REMEMBER 1.8.11. We found seats in the auditorium just as the program began.

Dr. Richard Carmona, a Tucson resident and a former

surgeon general of the United States, was the master of ceremonies. He began by asking us to pause and remember the nineteen citizens who had been attacked. He spoke about lessons learned from the tragedy and positive outcomes. Ron Barber had set up a Fund for Civility, Respect and Understanding, and a group of donors at U of A had established a scholarship fund in Christina-Taylor Green's name and mine for students interested in public service. There was talk of the event that had changed our lives on that "very dark and troubling day, when friends were senselessly mowed down." Pat Maisch spoke on behalf of the survivors and citizen heroes, and talked about the brave selflessness of ordinary citizens, the *first* first responders.

Afterward I hurried away with Kelly and my sisters, but a producer and reporter from Univision caught up with me and demanded a quick interview.

"Today's been a difficult day," I said, and I meant it. "We've learned lessons, I think, because of citizen heroes who stepped in and showed what the community of Tucson is all about."

The reporter asked me about Congresswoman Giffords, and I spoke about the remarkable progress she was making. And again they asked me about the first aid training I had received that had enabled me to help her a year before.

"Back in high school I received basic training in triage," I said. "I was able to run to Congresswoman Giffords. I knew I had skills she could use."

"What's next?" asked the reporter.

"I want to finish my university degree in May," I said, "and continue work in education sitting on the school board. I want to improve education in our community."

We shook hands, I thanked him, and we hurried along.

At Steve's house my parents had started setting up an informal buffet for a reception later. My dad was grilling chicken and hot dogs on the barbecue out in the backyard, and Alma helped my mom put out paper plates, bowls of guacamole, chips, salsa, and platters of tortillas and buns. We had a quick bite and then drove back to the university Mall for the candlelight vigil.

At the U of A, we sat in the front row closest to the raised stage. The stadium was packed with thousands of people. Everyone received a glow stick, but we waited to light them. It grew dark and cold.

Then Gabby walked onstage, with her husband Mark escorting her. The emcee, Ron Barber, said, "Welcome home, Congresswoman." We all cheered and applauded wildly. Everyone was still standing as Gabby led the Pledge of Allegiance. It was the first time I had seen her in person since the shooting. She had made tremendous progress in her recovery. Although she seemed to have limited motion of her right arm from her injury, she looked bright and was smiling. I hoped I would have a private minute with her while she was in Tucson.

The program began with music performed by the Tucson Symphony Orchestra. As they played "Hymn to the Fallen," nineteen candles were lit for those who had been shot. Gabby lit one of them. Then we cracked open our glow sticks and waved them to express support. The many speeches honored the victims and injured, and there were also expressions of hope for the future. Dr. Carmona applauded Tucson for thriving through a terrible tragedy. At the end of the vigil, as Gabby left the stage, people in the crowd shouted, "We need you, Gabby! We love you!"

I stayed awhile talking to Gloria and Spencer, Gabby's parents, and other good friends. Outside of the stadium TV reporters wanted to get my reactions, but I said, "No. I can't do interviews."

Back at Steve's house I hosted our informal gathering of people who had become so close because of the tragedy, Dr. and Mrs. Bowman, survivors, first responders, and different members of the community.

When I got up to speak, I said, "Today was a hard day for most of us 'framily' [the word Kelly had learned, a combination of "family" and "friend"]. I honestly wanted to say thank you all for stopping by. We'll keep seeing each other. We're a bunch that likes to talk and just talk."

Two days later I had a chance to see Gabby in her office before she left Tucson to return to Houston and rehab. She met with people one by one. I was the last to see her, and we had a few private minutes together. It was an emotional but important day, the conclusion of what we had all started a year before. The Congress on Your Corner event had fatefully tied all of us together for the rest of our lives.

I still don't think of myself as a hero. I was just a twenty-year-old intern who happened to be in the right place at the right time. I hope to dedicate myself to being a true hero someday, by doing something positive like Gabby has done, by helping others.

Daniel and Gabby meeting one year after the shooting

EPILOGUE

JANUARY 25, 2012, WAS A BITTERSWEET DAY. IT WAS MY TWENTY-second birthday and also the day on which Gabby officially resigned. She went from being congresswoman to former congresswoman. At home I watched the live feed from C-SPAN. I saw Gabby, as a member from the 8th Congressional District of Arizona, take her last vote on her bill to tighten drug laws along the border. Then her friend Representative Debbie Wasserman Schultz read Gabby's resignation letter aloud on her behalf, as Gabby stood quietly by. That moment ended an era of my life. I had gone from a seventeen-year-old naïve kid who had interned, to an adult who had been elected in his own right to fight for those who can't fight for themselves. I knew that I had expectations to fulfill, and a legacy to live up to.

I'm hanging on to the medallion that Gabby's mother loaned me, and I'll return it to Gabby someday when perhaps she goes back to work.

I kept thinking about what I had learned from the tragedy, something I'm often asked about wherever I travel. There are five lessons I think about on a daily basis. I don't want to sound too preachy, but I honestly believe that these are the lessons that I've learned from both the tragedy and my experiences so far.

First, the importance of education. Something a person learns, such as the first aid skills I acquired in high school and the training I received that enabled me to stay calm and collected, can help in a critical situation. Education has always been a great equalizer. It doesn't matter what your background is. If you have a good education, and if you work hard, you can get ahead.

Second, I realized the value of kindness. People often say that kindness is something that occurs by chance, and use the phrase "random acts of kindness," but in the past year I've learned there is no such thing. We should all purposely be doing little things all the time to be kind to people. Like being thoughtful, the way Gabe was when he made sure I had a cup of coffee that Saturday morning.

Third is the importance of civility. We must have constructive discourse, to make things better. Politics shouldn't be about destroying another person. We can't speak about the need for civility and then, in the next breath, attack someone for a position he or she holds. Fiery rhetoric and negative ads have become a winning strategy because we have not demanded more of ourselves as citizens, or of our elected officials as leaders. In light of January 8, civility gets talked about a lot. It won't happen overnight; we need to work toward it.

Fourth is the necessity of leadership. But that does not necessarily mean being in front. Leadership means having the knowledge and ability to step back and let others take the glory. Nelson Mandela, who served as president of South Africa, once said, "It is better to lead from behind and to put others in front, especially when you celebrate victory when nice things occur. You take the front line when there is danger. Then people will appreciate your leadership." Results matter more than credit. Sometimes working as a coalition proves more effective than acting as an individual.

Fifth, and probably most important, is public service, being involved, wanting to help others. On January 8 we lost many people who had served their community, from Judge John Rolls, a public servant in our justice system, to Phyllis Schneck, a volunteer in her church. There is no simple way of doing service. The main thing is getting off the sidelines and working to effect change.

Golda Meir, the former prime minister of Israel, is quoted as saying to her defense minister, Moshe Dayan, and perhaps to a visiting diplomat, "Don't be so humble; you're not that great." She may have said this in jest, but I have found her words exquisitely meaningful as I try to keep things in perspective. I've had the privilege of experiencing situations that no one my age might expect to have, from throwing the first pitch at an All-Star Game in Phoenix with baseball legend Joe Garagiola, to spending my twenty-first birthday at the White

House for the State of the Union address. I have strived to never let these wonderful opportunities get the better of me, and to stay grounded.

I have resisted the title of hero because I don't deserve it. My definition of "hero" is someone who has given of themselves in the service of others, like teachers, doctors, judges, and presidents. Becoming an active participant to create change is hard but vitally important, especially for those of us who live in groups that are marginalized: young, gay, Latino, Asian, African American, Native American, female, transgender, obese, physically or emotionally ill.

I have chosen to not be passive. I want to get up and fight for what is right, for myself and others like me. One day I hope to look back and say that I spent my life being an agent of change for the better. And then, maybe that day, I'll be able to think of myself as a hero.

WHERE THEY ARE NOW

Daniel Hernandez received his BA from the University of Arizona on May 12, 2012.

On August 8, 2012, Jared Loughner appeared for a plea hearing at the U.S. District Court in Tucson, Arizona. Daniel Hernandez and victims of the 2011 tragedy attended the hearing. Loughner pleaded guilty to killing six people and wounding thirteen others, and agreed to spend the rest of his life in prison. At a court hearing in Tucson on November 8, 2012, Loughner was sentenced to seven consecutive life sentences without parole, plus 140 years in prison. The case is closed.

Gabby continues to improve and is well enough to travel with her husband, Mark Kelly. They have moved back to the "Old Pueblo," Tucson, which was Gabby's dream after the shooting.

SPECIAL RECOGNITION AND AWARDS
FOR DANIEL HERNANDEZ

1. United States Office of Personnel Management Theodore Roosevelt Award for Outstanding Public Service
2. Presidential Citation by the League of United Latin American Citizens
3. Special recognition by Jan Brewer, governor of the state of Arizona
4. Special recognition on behalf of the country of Mexico, presented by the Mexican ambassador
5. Ceremonial first pitch at All-Star Game for Major League Baseball
6. Special proclamation from the New York City Council
7. National HOSA Heroes Award from the United States surgeon general
8. Special recognition by Mayor Michael Bloomberg of New York City
9. Sunnyside Alumni Association Learning Community Leader Award
10. Special citation by a county executive of Nassau County, Long Island
11. Arizona Hispanic Chamber of Commerce Courage and Distinction award

12. National Hispanic Media Coalition Impact Award for Outstanding Service to the Community
13. Aguila Youth Leadership Institute Mitch Menlove Public Servant Leadership Award
14. Gay & Lesbian Victory Fund award, Houston
15. Santa Rita Little League ceremonial first pitch
16. Hispanic Professional Action Committee Special Recognition Award for unselfish action and service to the community
17. Arizona HOSA Hall of Heroes award
18. Pima County Sheriff's Citizen Medal
19. University of Arizona 2011 Step UP! award
20. Campus Pride Voice and Action National Leadership Award
21. Citation by the Speaker of the California State Assembly
22. Sunnyside Unified School District citation
23. Special recognition by Latino Education and Advocacy Days
24. Good Deed Award by the Chabad Jewish synagogue, Mineola, Long Island
25. Special citation by Ed Perlmutter, member of Congress
26. Outstanding Recognition award by Pima County Foundation for Youth
27. Equality Forum's 2011 National Hero Award
28. San Diego LGBT Pride Parade grand marshal
29. Special recognition for Courage and Distinction (April 2, 2011) by the Tucson Hispanic Chamber of Commerce
30. Valle del Sol's Manuel Ortega Youth Leadership Award
31. Seattle Pride Parade grand marshal

HOW WE WROTE THIS BOOK

On May 15, 2011, I met Daniel Hernandez in Tucson, and we spent two days talking while I took notes. After that we spoke continually by phone so that I could understand his story and feel comfortable with his voice. I returned to Tucson on January 8, 2012, and stayed until January 11, taping interviews with Daniel. On February 3 we met in Los Angeles and I interviewed him for eight hours. After that, there were more long phone conversations, and e-mails back and forth.

I sent chunks of the first draft to Daniel on March 11, and he returned them with corrections and comments. By April 1, I had completed the first draft of the manuscript and sent it to him for his approval. On April 5, we submitted the draft to our editor, David Gale. When we received editorial notes we spoke again to answer David's queries. The last part of the book was the epilogue, which we finalized together. Our goal was to approximate Daniel's voice in telling his story.

ACKNOWLEDGMENTS

First, I thank Daniel Hernandez for entrusting his story to me, and working diligently with me to bring it to life. I also thank his parents, Daniel and Consuelo Hernandez, and his sisters, Alma and Consuelo, for welcoming me into their home and sharing reminiscences. I am enormously grateful to Kelly Paisley, who helped me from the start. I also want to thank Steve Farley and Carole Pearsall for their friendship and assistance.

I owe tremendous thanks to my editor, David Gale, for his immediate interest in this memoir, and for his hard work and guidance. My gratitude to the many people at Simon & Schuster who contributed their efforts, especially Navah Wolfe, Justin Chanda, and designers Chloë Foglia and Krista Vossen.

A huge thank-you to my agent and friend, George Nicholson, for suggesting this project and advising me along the way. My husband, Michael, gave me ongoing encouragement, and I am deeply grateful. Finally, special thanks to my friends, Michael Cart, and the writers of Lunch Bunch, for their generous suggestions.

—S. G. R.

Writing a memoir at any age can be difficult, particularly when I have so much more to do. But this was and continues to be a therapeutic and exciting adventure that I hope will help encourage other young people. Life has its ups and downs, but even in the darkest times there is hope, and we must always get up and keep going.

I would first like to thank my family. My mother, Consuelo; father, Daniel; and sisters, Alma and Consuelo. I would also like to thank my extended "framily": GiGi and Amelia Farley, Steve Farley, Jean and Jim Paisley, and David Pearsall. You have all become my rocks in the last two years that have empowered me to be the best I could be but also allowed me to remember what the important things in life are. You continue to be an inspiration for all that I do, and I don't often say it, but thank you! And I love you all very much. Words cannot explain how much you all mean to me.

I have to make a special mention of two members of my framily who have gone above and beyond from day one. Kelly Paisley and Carole Pearsall—you two have been my confidants and partners, from New York City all the way to Post, Texas. I truly appreciate it even if it doesn't always seem that way. You both push me to remember why I continue on this strange and wonderful journey.

I would like to thank Susan Goldman Rubin and the teams at Simon & Schuster and Sterling Lord: David Gale, Navah Wolfe, George Nicholson, Erica Silverman, Chloë Foglia, Paul

Crichton, and Anna McKean. You have all been great partners in this journey, and I've enjoyed all of our time together.

The victims and the heroes of January 8, 2011: You have all become so much more than friends—you are all family. Bill Badger and Sallie Badger, Pat Maisch, David and Nancy Bowman, John and Roxanna Green, Suzi Hileman, Mary Reed, Mavy Stoddard, Laura Tennen, Steven Rayle, and Faith and Roger Salzgeber.

Congresswoman Gabrielle Giffords, it is difficult to say how much you have impacted my life. I have always admired your strength, intelligence, and grace, but above all your humanity. I know that you are not done changing lives, and I hope to be able to continue to follow in your footsteps to serve the people of Arizona.

The family, supporters, and staff of Congresswoman Gabrielle Giffords have also been a strong system of support for me, and I will forever be grateful to all of you for your kindness. Mark Kelly, thank you for being such a great role model. Ron and Nancy Barber, like Mr. Kelly and Ms. Giffords, you both are examples of what it means to have a loving marriage, and I hope to one day find a partner whom I love as much as you love each other. Pam Harrington, my favorite strong-willed woman from Texas, you are one of the people I feel like I can be completely open and honest with, and I look forward to continued friendship. Pam Simon, your humor even in difficult times is something that I will always remember and cherish. Amanda Sapir and Patty Valera, I hope to one day find the sense of peace and strength you both have. You've found the balance between helping people and making sure you don't lose yourselves. Joni and Gary Jones, thank you for always having a caring hug and smile and for making me feel a part of the team. Mark Kimble and C. J. Karamargin, you both taught me so much about how to work with the press. Shay Saucedo and Dan Frey, I appreciate all the work you do for the people of southern Arizona. Rodd McLeod, simple thanks for teaching me so much about politics. Thank you to the DC and campaign staff—I didn't spend as much time as I would have wanted to get to know you all well, but I appreciated the times I got to spend with you. Thank you to Brad Holland and Gloria and Spencer Giffords for your kindness.

To Representative Debbie Wasserman Schultz, thank you for being so gracious every time we've interacted and for making me comfortable not with the word "hero" but with the word "mensch."

To my "sisters" from another mister: David Martinez III, Emily Fritze, Erik Lundstrom, Monica Ruiz, Chandni Patel, Shelby Vogl, Alicia Cybulski, Ashley Wilcox, Kirby Weatherford, Elma Delic, Abby and Beth Wischnia, Caitlin Brady, Laura Zimmerman, Carlita Cotton, Allison Coleman, Hillary Davidson, Jason Brown, Jenny Alexander, Martess Green, Kim Osesky, Ken Stroscher, Kenny Ho, and Laura Warbelow. You have shown me that all is possible with charisma, uniqueness, nerve, and talent. And that if I can't love myself, I can't love anyone else. You continually show me that sometimes all we need is a good cry at a restaurant at three a.m. or a sing-along in the car. Halleloo!

I would like to thank all of my teachers. Education has always been an integral part of my life, and one of the major reasons for this is the fact that I've been blessed to always have had such great instructors who have given me the tools I needed to succeed and never let me get away with anything less than the best: Ms. Katz, Ms. Martinez, Mrs. Jimenez, Mrs. Ybarra, Mrs. Breckenfeld, Ms. Rosales, Mr. Wyatt, Mrs. Diggins, Mrs. Bossardet, Mrs. Baca, Mrs. Winston, Mrs. Mayorga, Ms. Martin, Ms. Rush, Mrs. Monroe, Ms. MacDonald, Mr. Mayorga, Mrs. Heller, Mrs. Craft, Mr. Thames, Mr. Valenzuela, Mrs. Duarte, Mrs. Stewart, Mr. Dye, and Mrs. Gonzales. And my education would not have been complete without the support of the great people of Upward Bound and HOSA: Kristen Bury, Mike Lopez, and Jane Shovlin. A sincere and simple THANK-YOU.

In my new role as a school board member I have learned to even further appreciate the people who help give teachers the support that they need, so I give a thank-you to those who help me as I serve on the Sunnyside Unified School District Governing Board: Manuel and Edith Isquierdo, Dr. Eugenia Favela, Steve Holmes, Javier Baca, Anna Maiden, Mary Veres, Hector Encinas, Margie Jones, Eneida Orci, Liz Greenlee, Bernie Cohn, Kathy Dong, Dr. Bergman, Sue Tillis, and Gloria

Lopez. Also a thank-you to my fellow board members Malena Barajas, Eva Dong, Buck Crouch, and Louie Gonzales.

The other place where I thrived and learned was the University of Arizona. No other university has the incredible sense of community that is found there. I've built many friendships and received support I never expected from the people that work there. I will be a Wildcat for Life. That being said, I need to give a special thank-you to the staff who gave me a place in which to grow. Thank you to Melissa Vito, Robert Shelton, Meredith Hay, Pamela Coonan, Brint Milward, and Scott Johnson.

Special thanks to Chrissy Lieberman, Geoff Balon, Jen Dang, Khaled Sleiman, Michael Colletti, and Claudia Davila— you have seen me at my most vulnerable. You all helped me keep my head up high and my perspective in check.

My time in politics has been full of many wonderful people who I could never name even if I were given a thousand pages. Linda Quinn, Linda Lopez, Sabrina Vasquez, and Amanda Nelson, I feel like we are often on the same page and I always appreciate having someone I can talk to about anything. Nancy Young Wright and Cheryl Cage, I will always remember and cherish all the doors we knocked on and voters we talked to together. Representative Raúl Grijalva, thank you for standing up for southern Arizona and working to protect our beautiful home. Matt Heinz, you had confidence in me when I probably had no reason to think I knew what I was doing. Thank you for running my bill and helping the students of Arizona. Shasta McManus, you are hardworking and always deserve more recognition than you receive. I hope that we all tell you how appreciative we are of you. Adam Kinsey, you are always optimistic and honest—two things we need more of in politics. Bill Roe, thank you for your help immediately after the shooting and your service here in Arizona as Chair of the State Party. Fred Duval, thank you for your work in higher education as a regent; I hope to work with you more in the future to improve our state. And to two of my favorite Latinas: Linda Mazon Gutierrez and Christina Martinez. Thank you for always reminding me of my duty to help other young Latinos and to pay it forward.

Chris Herstam, Jack Jewett, Emily Rajakovich, Nancy Welch, Denise Eskildson, and all board members and staff of the Flinn and Thomas R. Brown foundations, a sincere thank-you for allowing me to be a Civic Leadership Academy Fellow to hopefully help improve things here in Arizona.

I have countless friends involved in public service who help make the country a better place: Kyrsten Sinema, Andrei and Stephanie Cherny, Regina Romero, Richard Fimbres, Jonathan Rothschild, Solomon Ortiz Jr., Macario Saldate, Chad Campbell, Linda Elliott, Vin Porfirio, Shane Windmeyer, Vic Basile, Terrie Gent, Teri Mills, Taylor Bell, Daniel Fitzgibbon, Sue Sissley, Sara Presler, Ruben Gallego, Rosanna Gabaldon, Robert Meza, Robyn Nebrich,

Paula Aboud, Olivia Cajero Bedford, Laura French, Mike Snitz, Luci Messing, Beth Slaine, Pat Burns, Matt Kopec, Curtis Dutiel, Jeannie Christie, Erin Hertzog, Rabbi Perl, Amethyst Polk, Bruce Wheeler, Carlos Menchaca, Serena Unrein, Mariana Garcia, Pat Fleming, Greg Stanton, Anna Tovar, Kelly Rivas, Loida De Leon, Melissa Vargas, Clare Velonis, Stephanie Gonzales, Justin Jenkins, Ruben Purdy, Patricia Strempel, Carlos Galindo, Katy Nail, Dyane Osorio, Jim Gonzales, Jonathan Cohen, Emily Berman, Teri Herbstman, Jesus Orozco, Christina Marie Rocks, Karolina Longoria, Courtney Frogge, David Turkell, Shayna Daitch, Frankie Parra, Jay Schlum, Diane Landis, Teri Benelli, Molly Edwards, Jeff Adams, Dino Kadich, Pedro Cavallero, Keri Silvyn, Deb Dale, Alfredo Garcia, Gabriela Rivera, Irvis Orozco, Denise Madrigal, Jonathan Beeton, Miguel Ortega, and Abby Henderson.

Tempest DuJour, Shangela, Janee' Starr, Jasmine White, and Barbara Seville, thanks for always making me smile.

There have been many organizations that I've had the pleasure of working with that I would like to thank: AIPAC, HRC, Campus Pride, NALEO, the Victory Fund, AEA, AEN, ASA, ASUA, USHLI, HWC, Valle del Sol, United Way, Council for Opportunity in Education, LPC, United States Hispanic Media Coalition, and Health Occupation Students of America.

—D. H.

BIBLIOGRAPHY

Books

Giffords, Gabrielle and Mark Kelly. *Gabby: A Story of Courage and Hope*. New York: Scribner, 2011.

Zoellner, Tom. *A Safeway in Arizona: What the Gabrielle Giffords Shooting Tells Us About the Grand Canyon State and Life in America*. New York: Viking, 2011.

Articles

Alaimo, Carol Ann. "Throughout Tucson, US, bells mark anniversary." *Arizona Daily Star*, January 9, 2012, pp. A1 and A5.

Beal, Tom. "January 8: One Year Later." *Arizona Daily Star*, Sunday, January 8, 2012, Section C, p. 5.

Bond, Gavin. "The 2011 OUT100, Daniel Hernandez Jr. Hero." *OUT*, December 2011/January 2012, p. 77.

Gonzalez, Daniel. "Tucson Tragedy Three Months Later: Public Faces, Private Pain." *The Arizona Republic*, April 3, 2011, pp. A1 and A8.

———. "Giffords' intern struggles to cope with Arizona tragedy." *The Arizona Republic*, April 4, 2011.

Herreras, Mari and Jim Nintzel. "The Heroes: January 8: One Year Later." *Tucson Weekly*, January 5–11, 2012, vol. 28, no. 46, p. 21.

Martindale, Scott. "Intern who saved Rep. Giffords honored in Anaheim." *The Orange County Register*, June 22, 2011.

Rose, Jaimee and Mary Jo Pitzl. "Daniel Hernandez, intern, stays by Gabrielle Giffords' side." *The Arizona Republic*, January 9, 2011.

Wallace, Amy. "I Heard the Shots and Ran Toward the Sound." *GQ*, March 2011.

Internet

Constantini, Cristina. "Daniel Hernandez Jr., Gabrielle Giffords' Hero Intern, On Anniversary of Tucson Shootings." The Huffington Post, Latino Voices, January 7, 2012, http://huffingtonpost.com/2012/01/06/Daniel-hernandez-jr-hero-intern_n_1190394.html

Crites, Nicole. "Giffords' intern thought she was dead as he waited in sequester." January 6, 2012, http://www.kpho.com/story/16463389/giffords-intern-thought-she-was-dead-as-he-waited-in-sequester

Gonzalez, Daniel. "Intern Daniel Hernandez to be honored at State of the Union." *The Arizona Republic*, January 24, 2011, http://www.azcentral.com/news/articles/2011/01/24/20110124gabrielle-giffords-david-hernandez-state-union.html

Johnson, Chris. "Gay intern credited with saving Giffords." *Washington Blade*, January 13, 2011, http://www.washingtonblade.com/2011/01/13/openly-gay-man-credited-with-saving-gifford/

Maldonado, Trisha. "Former Gifford's intern visits Douglas students." *Douglas Dispatch*, February 8, 2012, http://www.douglasdispatch.com/articles/2012/02/23/news/doc4f32dfd7da6d9418256096.txt

Myers, Amanda Lee. "Photo Shows Giffords Right Before Shooting Rampage." March 4, 2011, http://www.aolnews.com/2011/03/04/photo-shows-rep-gabrielle-giffords-right-before-shooting-rampag/

Phillips-Sandy, Mary. "Daniel Hernandez Celebrates 21st Birthday at State of the Union Address." January 25, 2011, http://www.aolnews.com/2011/01/25/daniel-hernandez-celebrates-21st-birthday-at-state-of-the-union/

Portillo Jr., Ernesto. "Neto's Tucson: Even as a child, Daniel Hernandez was calm, poised." *Arizona Daily Star*, January 16, 2011, http://azstarnet.com/news/local/neto-s-tucson-even-as-a-child-daniel-hernandez-was/article_8a793cdb-7149-59a8-b360-659c00df1f69.html

Powers, Ashley. "Former Giffords intern elected to Arizona school board." *Los Angeles Times*, November 10, 2011, http://articles.latimes.com/2011/nov/10/nation/la-na-daniel-hernandez-20111110

Washington Post editors. "Tucson shooting timeline: Pima Sheriff's Office." *The Washington Post*, January 14, 2011, http://voices.washingtonpost.com/44/2011/01/tucson-shooting-timeline-pima.html

Wright, John. "Gay intern credited with saving Giffords' life." Dallasvoice.com, January 9, 2011, http://www .dallasvoice.com/meet-gay-intern-saved-rep-giffords-life-1060085.html

Interviews Conducted by the Author via E-mail

Alma Hernandez to Susan Goldman Rubin, March 19, 2012.

Consuelo Hernandez to Susan Goldman Rubin, February 2, 2012.

Kelly Paisley to friends after the shooting, January 15, 2011.

Kelly Paisley to Susan Goldman Rubin, February 7, 2012, and March 31, 2012.